ALCHERINGA

When the First Ancestors were Created

Valerie J Barrow

First published in 2002 by Vishruti Prints, India.
Second edition published in 2014 by Custom Books

This edition published in Australia by Aurora House
www.aurorahouse.com.au

This edition published 2020
Copyright © Valérie Judith Barrow 2020
www.valeriebarrow.com

Typesetting and e-books: Amit Dey
Cover design: Simon Critchell
Illustrations: Simon Weir and Bob Wright

ISBN number: 9781922403056 (paperback)

A catalogue record for this book is available from the National Library of Australia

Distributed by: Ingram Content: www.ingramcontent.com

Australia: phone +613 9765 4800 |
email lsiaustralia@ingramcontent.com

Milton Keynes UK: phone +44 (0)845 121 4567 |
email enquiries@ingramcontent.com

La Vergne, TN USA: phone +1 800 509 4156 |
email inquiry@lightningsource.com

*"The day science begins to study non-physical phenomena,
it will make more progress in one decade, than in all
previous centuries of its existence"*

~ Nikola Tesla

This book is dedicated to the light being known as *Alcheringa*, residing at Uluru, and to the ancient Aboriginal Spirit of the Earth.

We visited the great Rock ULURU at the centre of Australia.

We heard of the Indigenous 'Dreaming' story held 'forever' by them, of the 'seven sisters from the Pleiades' and they being the Ancestors of the Indigenous people of Australia.

This photo was taken by the author, Valerie J Barrow when she visited Uluru and called upon Goolagia, the Black Giantess who has been holding the story on Earth of the Eighth Sister returning.

The huge magenta orb represents Goolagaia the Eighth Sister, and she is surrounded by Seven Sisters, Rainbow Orbs as told in the Legend. At the top was first seen an Eagle, and then the huge White Orb from the World of Light - it is not the sun.

Hieroglyphs at Kariong near Gosford N.S.W. Australia

CONTENTS

AUTHOR'S NOTE

In general terms, the concept of reincarnation is accepted by the Eastern and Indigenous cultures. As time goes forward, it is also being accepted by many of our Western cultures, where there is a belief that our spirit, our soul, lives on after death and returns into a new body to continue its journey of character building until we reach enlightenment. This is referred to as 'past life memory' of being another personality in another life, sometimes as male sometimes female - it is all written into our soul history.

In the story told in this book, we have found that many people reach into an initiated state of conscious where they experienced 'past life memories' of living in another body, but the consciousness reaches into their soul to release the memory of being from other worlds; from other planets.

For these people written about in this book, the transition into Cosmic Consciousness was relatively easy. Their memories were sparked by looking at symbols, which communicated with us at a deep level for I am one of those who remember.

Carl Jung, the famous psychologist speaks about the archetypes and the collective unconscious. This is particularly illustrated with many artists portraying archetypal sacred geometry in their artwork. Sometimes hypnotherapy is used to access this hidden consciousness. For our spiritual aspirants the knowledge, the memories, came from merely looking at and feeling the very simple symbolic glyphs cut into a stone wall. The hidden knowledge within each of them was released spontaneously.

This leads us to believe there was a 'hidden hand' at work guiding us all to release one segment of the story, after another that is from a collective consciousness. It is the story of when the upstanding ape-like creature was elevated into a human being. A man of Light.

This is our story. How it unfolded is a true story. We have used only some of the transcripts from the audio tapes and dramatised them slightly for easy reading. I still have the audio tapes, recorded from the different people sitting, holding photos of the glyphs and remembering that time in earth's past history.

We have changed the people's names to protect their identity but many of them have agreed to allow a group photo to be published. Until the sitting for the photo, many of the 'story tellers' in this combined narrative had not yet met one another.

Sri Sathya Sai Baba personally blessed the first 'Book of Love by a Medium' saying, "It is not finished yet", and who again blessed the second manuscript 'Alcheringa, When the First Ancestors were Created' which told the real story. Sai Baba called it "The Booku".

This is the story of fifty thousand people coming from the Pleiades in a giant star ship to found the human race on Earth, and to free the existing race of Hairy Ones from Reptilian mind control.

The mystery started when Valerie Barrow received a little stone wrapped in paper bark. Known by the Australian Aboriginal people as an 'Alcheringa Stone', it enabled Valerie to communicate with an unseen being who identified himself as having the same name as the stone - Alcheringa.

It is not a simple story, but one filled with intrigue, deception, and the planned destruction of a mission that left only ninety survivors to be cast upon the Earth. Their struggle and success in creating our race is the miracle they wrought. It is our past. They are our heritage.

The Aboriginal people have known this all along. It was a gift from the Star People.

The gift of this book is that it foretells a New Age where life will be completely different. With changes coming there is a way to survive. This book tells how. It is remarkably simple.

INTRODUCTION

How do I tell you about extra-terrestrial events that took place almost a million years ago without you thinking that I belong in the nearest mental hospital?

Many people have come to me to recall memories of these distant events, quite normal people who live regular lives.

It was easy for me to accept what these people told me. I've had firsthand recall experiences of my own that correspond closely with the information they gave.

The reader of this book may or may not think so.

Many people experience distant recall events and write extensively about them. Some who have them choose not to talk about it at all. Others just ignore it all together, putting it down to a vivid imagination, or not wanting to know.

Memories of past lives become very real when they are triggered by some special event. They can appear alarmingly similar to events, relations, and attitudes of your current life. These memories can change your life forever.

That's exactly what happened to my life.

Now I have a mission to tell people of the distant past, and convey the information given to me by others. This is to help bring an understanding of who and what we really are. That is what this book is about.

I ask you to just read and observe this little book. Please don't make a judgment, not until the end anyway. For a little while, allow yourself to look at another kind of reality...

It all started when I looked up the word *alchemy* in the dictionary. My husband and I were deciding on a name for our new home. I was trying out some ideas.

As I turned to the page, it wasn't alchemy that caught my eye. It was Alcheringa, the next entry. The dictionary said the Australian Aboriginal word meant 'The Dreamtime,' 'The Golden Age,' or 'When the first ancestors were created.' We liked it, and our home came to be known as Alcheringa.

Then along came Helen Boyd. A friend told her about me, and that I lived at a place called Alcheringa. She came to see me bringing a stone wrapped in the bark of the paper bark tree. Helen was seriously ill and wanted to find a safe place to keep the stone.

An Afghanistan family had given the stone to Helen. They knew the stone was special, but didn't know what to do with it. In early days, traders from Afghanistan travelled the central Australian desert selling goods that they hung from their camels, a type of general store on four legs. No one knows how the stone came into the family's possession.

Helen said the stone was called an 'Alcheringa stone'. Her Aboriginal friends told her that's what it was. Helen said my house was also called Alcheringa, and that was the reason she had come to see me. She decided that I could be trusted, and asked if I would watch over the stone.

I said okay, and without blinking an eye, Helen left the stone in my care. It fit quite nicely into a shoebox. I put it on a bookshelf in my study.

Many weeks later, I woke to the sound of a disembodied voice asking me, "Are you ready to write a book?"

In a panic, I sat upright, feeling the presence of someone next to me. "Book, what book, who are you?" I yelled.

My husband grunted, and rolled over in his sleep. It certainly wasn't him doing the talking. In the centre of my head, the new voice continued, explaining it was a *Being of Light* who came from a different dimension that I could not readily see, a place of unity, harmony, and love.

The voice was soothing and friendly. While it was inside of me, it seemed separate and real. I thought to myself, *What is this?*

The voice answered, "I am *Alcheringa*."

A rush of realisation hit me, I had just communicated mentally with something named Alcheringa on the other side. This was not a bad dream or an out of control imagination.

So, I thought about this for some time. I also thought about the Alcheringa stone in the shoe box, the name of our house, and a few million other things.

I had zero confidence in writing a book, not to mention what I could write about. For several weeks, I walked around thinking about 'things' to write. Nothing occurred to me, there was no light of realisation. My typewriter sat cold and lifeless on my desk.

The little shoebox caught my eye. I sat on the floor and took the wrapped stone out of the box, sat it in my lap and looked at it. It seemed to have a life of its own, radiating a feeling of light and love. Everything was very quiet for the first few moments that I sat with it. I found myself without any thought process at all.

There was a shift. My consciousness moved from my head into my heart, and the entity Alcheringa spoke again. Only this time, he spoke using my vocal chords, in a voice quite unlike my own.

"I am Alcheringa, a being of light. You yourself are an aspect of a being of light. In coming to you, I have adjusted my vibration so that I can speak through your physical body. This is just a little theatre so that you and others around you can witness the reality of beings that exist in other dimensions. In my reality, I come from a point in which I cannot frequent this place. I must work through someone such as yourself to make my presence known.

"There are many things I could tell you, but for now I will speak about energy. I would suggest that you ask questions, and know that when you do ask questions, you are communicating with energy from other worlds and dimensions. I would encourage you to become familiar with the feeling of this energy, for this is the essence of my being. Do you understand?"

"I'm not so sure that I do," I gasped.

"Soon you will. Long ago, you made a decision to come to this time and place. There is a feeling within that draws you here. It is like a magnetic energy that is familiar. This is because you connected with this world at another time. That is the reason for your coming, and deep inside you know this. I invite you to feel and know that understanding from within. If you will call upon me, I will help you to understand this, and to know that there is work for you to do.

"I will not tell you too much in the beginning because you may get off on a little track of your own. Some of the work needs to be delayed for a while until one thing falls into place with another. Do you understand?"

I shook my head, "No, what do you mean?"

"Sometimes it will be necessary for you to join with others. Their path has also been delayed so that you will come together at the right time. I ask you to follow your direction from within. If you feel good about this, then keep going.

"Remember, the light that you walk in on this Earth is one of experience. Do not miss any of it, even for a moment, for it is a journey that will be very important. Those who have committed to work with us on this Earth are truly loved, and we work very willingly with them. We have a bigger picture, a plan that is unfolding around the Earth.

"Others like you are helping to actuate this plan. But one must not rush too far ahead of the others, or the plan will not happen as it is meant to be. I hope this reassures you my dear, I trust that you feel you are in the right place."

There was a little pushing sensation inside, making me want to find out more.

"How many of you are doing this?" I asked.

"There are many like myself whose energies are upon the Earth at this time. We work with some who do not even realise it at a conscious level. This does not matter. It is the intent and the light that matters. You are one of those who will know of us. With much love in my heart, I will now take my leave. I thank you for welcoming me, and God bless you."

I could feel the subtle energy that was Alcheringa's being pulling away, leaving me with an exhilaration that I will never ever forget. What remained was the new feeling, the pushing sensation that compelled me to get on with a job of which I had no concept.

One of the first things he communicated was knowledge that the Alcheringa stone was brought to Earth by an extra-terrestrial culture known as the 'Star People'. The stone was given to the original Aboriginal people of what is now Australia. It is sacred to them. In coming away from their keeping, it is on a journey to influence many others. It teaches of our spiritual beginnings, and imparts knowledge that is ethereally written into it.

The stone felt familiar to me. I knew in my heart that it was destined to come to me for a purpose. This was first realised when I completed the manuscript.

The Book of Love by a Medium was published in Hong Kong. It was written in the style of a diary, a stream-of-consciousness record. Much of it came through the entity Alcheringa with the assistance of the Alcheringa stone. The book spoke of the star people and their mission to Earth.

Then came a dream in which I saw Sai Baba, a Holy Man dressed in white, standing beside me as I was writing. There was a strong feeling that I should take the book to India in the hope he would personally bless it.

My husband and I travelled to India and found many thousands of people at his ashram. Yet he called us for an interview, and asked for the book. Holding it in his lap he looked at me with smiling eyes and said, "The book is not finished."

Then came a series of events that changed everything. As they unfolded, I realised that I had only described a part of the story in my first book.

Now I have to do it all over again.

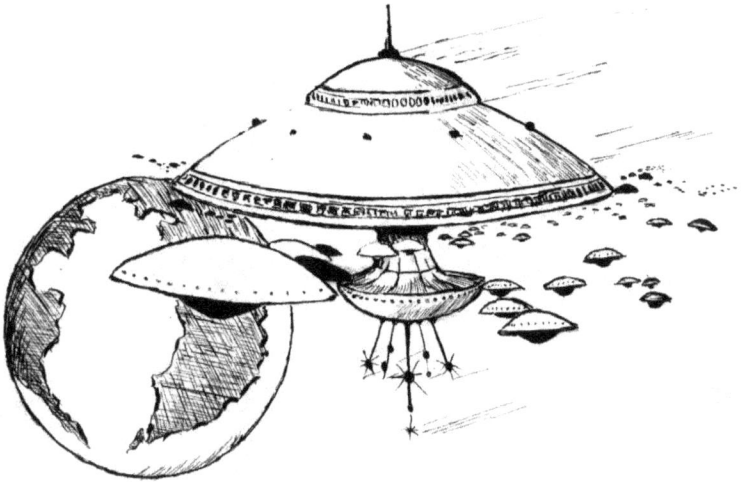

The Mothership Rexegena

Overview

The Mothership was raised on the eighth planet of the Pleiadean cluster in the constellation of Taurus. It was built, in our terms, quite differently from what the earthling understands at this time. It was a crystalline body. It had a consciousness because of the crystal, a consciousness that had been imbued into it by its builders. It actually grew. Liquid crystal is used in many ways to make many things in the star peoples' dimension.

The huge mothership was formed and then mounted by the appointment of a Commander-in-chief known as Alchquaringa. His wife was named Egarina. There were other Commanders on the ship – and divisions of command within the ship. Those that came on the Mission had love and compassion in their hearts.

They came because the Hierarchy, similar to your United Nations, had put out a call for help to be taken to this corner of the galaxy where dark, heavy, negativity resided. Many volunteers came from other planetary systems, with their families, knowing their journey would be a long one.

The objective of the Mission was to bring New Beings to this Earth, to help raise the consciousness of the earth. They had hoped to breed among themselves and that the progeny from the star people would be introduced genetically to intermingle with the up-standing apelike creature who already existed upon the earth. Genetic engineering was well known and understood by the star people. The mission was to save the animal people on this earth, who were under mind control. The mind control came from beings not of love and compassion. They were known as the Reptilian people, for they were genetically connected to snakes and lizards as we know them. The Reptilian people controlled the up-standing apelike creature and used them at their will.

The objective was not only to free the animal man from slavery, but also to stop them being used in sacrifice to Draconian Gods. There had been those appointed as Diplomats from the Hierarchy to come to speak with the Reptilian Kingdom and try to find a way for them to release the animal man. It was the Hierarchy's understanding the Reptilian Kingdom had agreed to hand over the earth to the people who came on the Mission. They in turn would leave. There had been an amount of discussion and concessions made, but this was the outcome; at least that is what was believed.

50,000 people on the Mothership came, fully believing the reptilians would leave. A handover ceremony took place, but it was a complete sham. The reptilian people had no intention of leaving the earth. Nor did they have any intention of stopping the slavery and sacrifice that existed upon this earth. The Star people could not believe anyone could say something and not mean it.

When the Mothership arrived with the new race, the reptilians attacked it, even though it was completely defenceless, blowing it out of the sky. Only a few managed to escape. Those who survived established a small community in the southern hemisphere. The Mothership exploded above the area that exists now around Jerusalem.

There was to be a Jerusalem established by the star people. Jerusalem means that the star people were to intermingle with the slave-like people and teach them love and compassion. A dualism. The star people, the survivors, found it too difficult because of the heavier atmosphere; they had difficulty breathing and found the sun was far too hot. They tried to introduce genetic change to their own progeny, creating hair on their heads, stronger lung systems and stronger digestive systems to avoid disease. These children did not live; the gestation period was not long enough in the new atmosphere.

The star people decided to genetically engineer the upstanding ape-like creature. Genes from the star people were intermingled with the animal man embryo, then implanted into the females. The babies were born with a larger skull, a little less hair, which went on then to evolve so the more children born, the less hair was manifested. It was the time the scientists speak of as the missing link. It was a time when the star people first introduced fire and showed the animal-like being – now the human – how to cook food to lessen their vulnerability to disease, to teach them the knowledge of the

Creator of All. To teach them more about the star people, how they live as family and how they married. They taught them how to communicate telepathically, and other clever things similar to the star people. They also taught them to honour and care for their Mother Earth.

This original race was known by the star people as `The Chosen Ones' who were the ancestors of the indigenous people. The indigenous people still carry this knowledge and understanding in their mythology. As the original numbers grew, the star people took them out around the earth and told them to multiply with other upstanding ape-like creatures who were still brutish and weapon wielding. The change from the animal man to hu-man began to uplift the consciousness of those beings along with strict marriage laws so that they did not interbreed. The star-people eventually died, but not before telling the Australian Indigenous People they would return one day.

And they have.

The Technology

With the star peoples' technical ability they were able to make the Mothership grow into the magnificent 'state of the arc' piece of equipment.

The mothership Rexegena inside is completely white, very clean cut and not much furniture. Just long, rounded, smooth to touch moulded seats, slightly shiny, along the side of walls, again all white.

There are rooms off corridors in the `sleeping section' where everything is very quiet. Inside the room, lights and furniture are available by waving the hand over a small point on a wall, like a light switch, with 'thought in mind' opening the bed section for instance, or turning on a soft light. The bed appears as the section of the wall opens. It is more like a cylinder the star person climbs into, after removing boots, and mentally closing the see-through cover over their body. The air inside is stabilised into an atmosphere that allows the star person to sleep for whatever time chosen. It could even be for the full time of travel until the destination is almost reached. The star person's mind is then linked to the mothership so as to assist its pre-programmed course. There are always certain numbers of star people that are on 'watch'. Meaning they are in a suspended state of mind to focus only on the movement of the mothership. Fifty thousand people are on board, with never a feeling of over-crowding.

At the top of the mothership is the Command Deck, about twenty people move about purposefully. It operates with extremely advanced computer technology. The Deck itself is large and mostly surrounded with windows, taking in a magical view of the galaxy. Large movie screens hang like thin pictures on the remaining walls, which light upon command, showing star maps of where the ship is located, where it has been and where it is going.

To operate these star screens, there are coloured desktop directional control mechanisms. Some of these are buttons as you would use on a computer, others are like a half globe coloured light set into a console, that when the star person passes a hand over it adjusts the pathway of the mothership on its journey. A circular shelf used as a desk links all the technical line ways within the ship right around the window area surrounding three-quarters of the circular command platform.

At the back of the command room, and in front of the star screens, is a large white moulded desk at which the Commander-in-Chief sits. His seat has a narrow rather high back showing the Shiva symbol in red and black. The huge desk also doubles as a kind of boardroom seating place for his Commanders when they meet to discuss issues about operating the mothership or other matters.

Eight robots converse with the crystal consciousness on the ship. I see one of them seated on a moulded white seat in front of a panel placing disks, like CD's, into slots at eye level. This also has an influence on the maintenance of the ship and its programming. The robots have an eye only for a face, which can move in all directions. The body is like coiled rope of a satin stainless steel-looking material. It has arms, with a tiny hand and long fingers. The legs taper onto a circular platform. The Robot glides slightly above the floor. Each robot is operated by a communication crystal at the instruction of one of the commanders. The core of the whole mothership is flowing liquid crystal, which virtually powers the ship, also allowing the star people to regenerate their own body cells. The ship could be described as organic.

On the lower floor of the mothership are gardens, plant life that look more teal in colour than green. There are bathing pools, waterfalls, playful lights and soft sounds to induce relaxation, and parklands as well as heavier forestation. All of this is to encourage the star people to relax and intermingle for not all onboard are from the same planet, although they all come voluntarily with love and compassion in their heart.

One floor is devoted to genetic research; the rooms are white and sterile. The star people are not subjected to bacteria or fungus. There have been some children born onboard.

They are placed in an upright cylinder, with a controlled atmosphere, allowing each child to develop fully. The parents nurture their child with telepathic communication and love, as well as mother's milk. There are star women on board who devote their work to midwifery. Care is taken to analyse the new-born children in their progression both physically and consciously before they are mature enough to leave the cylinder.

Understand that the dimension on which the mothership exists would be the fifth dimension, with frequency adjustment made to the fourth dimension as the ship passed through the gateway of change on its way to the four dimensional earth or *Mu,* as it was known.

Another floor is for the development of botanical research. Taking up a lot of space and grown as we would understand hydroponics, the water being a flowing liquid crystal, giving off a fresh smell and a gentle humidity.

The mothership deals with maintaining the mechanics of the ship on yet another floor. Most of the star people are dressed in navy-coloured boiler suits and boots or pearl silvery-white boiler suits, and boots – depending upon their race or position.

On other floors are lounge rooms, large gathering halls for celebrations or events and a kind of film library.

Star people mainly take liquids but some like sweet cake-like food, which is never over eaten. Overweight is not a problem – people know and understand what their body needs to be sustained. There is more body contact and interaction than one could imagine with aliens. Communication is telepathic, with a lot of body language as well. Permission to speak is always asked first, and is telepathic. From our earth point of view, their physical body looks anorexic, but it is a perfectly healthy body.

The spaceship has a hospital on board. Light and sound technology is used for healing as well as genetic engineering. Use of this technology is an everyday occurrence but only ever with the view of transforming a body with permission from The Creative Source.

A childcare centre is onboard as well. Dancing occurs with people holding hands, like the Greeks or Jewish people dance, moving the feet so that they skip quite fast at times, and moving around in large circles, according to the music. These dances are enjoyed and happily shared. From the outside, not much emotion is witnessed but from the inside star people actually experience emotion much more acutely and strongly than the earthlings.

On meeting, one hand is placed across the chest as a greeting. Closer friends may raise their hands and actually give what we would call a 'high five'. Intimate relationships stand in front of each other – palm to palm of both hands, fingers touching so as to connect with all of each other's meridians. This is always exciting and pulls at the heart. They sometimes put an arm around another or even give each other a hug.

A storage area take up a whole floor. It has vast supplies to be used when the fifty thousand people establish the new settlement on Earth.

There are also flight decks that hold different types of flying ships. Many ships are used as surveillance vehicles. They can hold as many as fifty people. Others are smaller and are used to traverse more areas that are difficult, or landing locations. There are also fifty hand-flying scooters.

To offload material from the ship onto land a chute is used – operated by one person in a small rocket-looking flying ship, or pod.

There are no weapons of destruction on board – the mothership is completely defenceless.

There are other Flying Ships used by the Leonine people and the Reptilian people.

These two races are sworn enemies. Both have weapons of destruction. The Leonine ships are larger than the Reptilians'. The light onboard is not bright white like the star people's mothership. Their technology is not as advanced, although by earthling standards that exist at the present, their technology is far more advanced. The ships are described as untidy compared to the bright white mothership. Furniture is on display and covered with skins – not tucked away as designed on star ships. Both races dress in military-style uniforms.

Both races have ray guns that can 'freeze' whatever it is pointed at. They use sonic equipment to destroy, the same way a high-pitched sound can smash glass. Only the sonic sound is entrained so that it continues to destroy objects until they no longer exist.

This is what happened when the Reptilians set out to destroy the huge mothership. Portions of the mothership were destroyed, blow after blow, but it did give time for the star people to move quickly to the surveillance ships enabling them to escape. When the fleeing ships left and tried to fly away, they were also attacked. Only a few ships managed to escape from the Reptilian line of fire.

One of the robots was rescued and survived along with ninety other star people.

The star people had what was called a laser rod. It did everything. It enabled them to lift or levitate, make changes in work, shape and burn. Not with heat that would harm. It would solidify or liquefy. Make something softer, and transform material into another material. It was also what was used to cut into stone. Very useful. I know that also they had a boomerang shaped instrument, which of course was explained to and used by the Cherished Ones.

All of these events operated in the fourth dimensional frequency of Earth time. It was only later in Earth's evolution – about 12,000 years ago at the catastrophic time of the Great Flood or the Fall of Atlantis – that the Earth fell into the third Dimensional frequency.

A Green Crystal ... the Moldavite Stone

In earlier days, when we first moved to the Southern Highlands, I was awakened from a deep sleep and asked by a voice from 'upstairs' to 'find a green crystal'.

I thought that was strange, as I had never seen a green crystal. Always dutiful to my spiritual guidance I decided to travel to Sydney on other errands, but also with intention to call into a well-established 'Esoteric Bookshop' where I knew crystals were sold. Later, upon arriving at the shop I asked the owners if they had any green crystals. To my surprise they presented to me a tray of smallish green crystals they called a Moldavite glass stone. I was advised it was actually a tektite that came from outer space and was only found near the Moldau River in Czechoslovakia.

Gazing at the tray of stones, one caught my eye as if it was saying, 'Pick me, Pick me.' As I lifted the small stone toward me I was overcome with a blinding white light and a strong male disembodied voice spoke to me, saying, "You are going home."

Going home? What on earth was he speaking about. I was shaking badly and had to sit down – the shopkeeper was concerned about my reaction and ushered me to a chair. In fact, she suggested I lie on a massage table in another room until I recovered. She also said that it is not the first time someone has had a reaction to these moldavite stones.

It took about an hour for me to steady myself. I found the stone was a seventeen-carat stone and the cost added to seventeen – my birthday is on the seventeenth so I considered that to be a sign and decided to buy it. I still could not touch the stone – so the understanding shopkeeper wrapped it in a box and placed into my handbag.

It was several weeks before I could actually hold it, introducing the energy of the stone to myself, touching it with one finger only, until it felt comfortable.

This experience was in 1986. It was not until I received the Aboriginal sacred stone in 1994 and the stories that followed from then, did I realise that the message I received, 'I was going home' was referring to a memory from my soul being a Star Person and coming from the Pleiades in the huge Mother-ship Rexegena. That story told of fifty thousand Star people coming to Earth in Peace – to hold Divine Light on this Earth and to assist in creating hairy men into a Hu-man – meaning a 'Light man'.

My recent research suggests the Moldavite stone is also known as the 'Grail Stone', or 'Starborn Stone'.

Scientists say that millions of years ago there was a meteorite shower, and this rare, bottle-green crystal was the result. It belongs to a group of tektites, which are fragments of extraterrestrial objects such as meteorites and the ensuing melted combination with terrestrial rocks when they crash to the earth.

Moldavite is named for an area of Czechoslovakia in which a large crater field was discovered. They are among the most rare minerals on earth, rarer than diamonds, emeralds, or rubies, and prized by humans for thousands of years.

According to legend, the clear, deep green stone in the Holy Grail was Moldavite. and anyone who touches the 'Grail Stone' will have a spiritual transformation. This stone activates the 'dream states' and is said to induce positive life changes and also helps widen our cosmic consciousness. It is helpful for personal and spiritual growth, and to release old habits that you know, deep down, need to go.

I certainly have gained cosmic consciousness and now I am able to assist others to connect to theirs.

I have a memory of the Mothership Rexegena when I had a dream witnessing it exploding portion by portion after it had been attacked. In my memory, and many other people's memory, the Mothership was stationed on the outer atmosphere of this planet earth. The ship was organic. With the Star people's technical ability they were able to make it grow into the magnificent state-of-the-art piece of equipment when it was raised on the eighth planet of the constellation of the Pleiades.

The explosion in my dream looked like a nuclear explosion – hotter than the sun, causing the Mothership to melt. Many onboard perished.

IT WOULD HAVE FALLEN TO EARTH, and this is what is now named the Moldavite Stone. Our memory tells us some of it's remains went into water and some onto land – mainly around Bohemia and Moravia, of the Czech Republic. This word comes from the Greek word tektos, which means 'melted' and was first employed by the geologist Franz Sues in the year 1900.

When I was first awakened by Spirit and asked to find 'a green crystal' I had no idea they existed, let alone the story that has since unfolded about The Mothership Rexegena.

Czech moldavites hold an especially significant position among other tektites. They are the only tektites that are transparent – glass-like and that stand out with a variety of green shades.

I do not find it difficult to accept the Mothership melted and fell to earth, and that the dating of the Moldavite Stone could be confusing unless it was accepted that the Stone was Star Man made and hence needing a different approach in Earthman's scientific expertise.

As previously mentioned, the Mothership existed in the fifth dimension with frequency adjustment made to the fourth dimension as the ship passed through the gateway of change on its way to the four dimensional earth.

Entrance to Cave at Kariong

Anubis

Pregnant Starlady

CHAPTER 1

Valerie Goes to Kariong
with Gerry and Karen

It's a little overwhelming when I think about what took place.

Aborigine Gerry Bostock raced his battered pickup truck down a dirt trail towards the highway. My friend Rachel sat beside him, her white knuckles clenching the dashboard. As Gerry drove, he admired an unusual pink crystal he had just bought.

Approaching the highway, Gerry brought the truck to a stop. The dirt trail ahead was covered with huge concrete pipes. A construction crew member, laying them in the deep trench that ran across the trail, noticed the truck through a cloud of brown dust. All he could do was smile and shrug his shoulders. Another way would have to be found to the highway.

As Gerry searched for an alternative route, his truck neared the road that leads to the happy place my husband and I call home. Rachel pointed at the road, "That's where my friend Valerie lives, her home is called Alcheringa."

Gerry slowed the truck and then stopped at the crossing. For a moment, he looked intently down the narrow lane. He turned to Rachel, "Then we will go and see her." The attraction of the name Alcheringa was about to pull in yet another new acquaintance.

In my little study, I sat with the Alcheringa stone having a small celebration. Today, the first copies of *The Book of Love by a Medium* (that's me) arrived in Australia. I was happy and content.

Through the window, I could see an old pickup truck approaching the house. I recognized my friend Rachel in the truck along with an Aboriginal man. As I saw his face, I felt a strong rush of excitement that I was unable to justify.

Like many Australians, I had never met a 'Koori' or 'Murri', as they like to be called. When I say this, I feel sad. I was born and raised in Australia, yet never took the opportunity to meet the Koori socially. This is the same for many white Australians. It is hard for them to take the initiative.

There is a great need to have communication and understanding between all races at a social level. My chance had just arrived and I decided to make the most of it.

Rachel beamed as she introduced me to Gerry. I looked through his dust-covered eyeglasses to see the warmest pair of brown eyes I had ever seen. His smile was gigantic and sincere. There was a feeling of love and niceness about him.

I instantly connected with him and felt warm to his energy. As I did, he looked deeper into my eyes than anyone ever had before.

I made lunch, and as we sat at the table, I intuitively felt that Gerry knew the Alcheringa stone was in my care. My gaze moved to Rachel for a clue, but if she had told Gerry about it, her face was certainly not revealing anything to me.

We talked socially for a while, and then Rachel asked Gerry to show me the crystal he had just bought. As he reached into his pocket, Rachel told me that Gerry used crystals in his work as a healer. Gerry brought the pink crystal forth and held it out to me. He looked right into my eyes.

"It's a magic stone is it not?"... I almost fainted.

"You know about the Alcheringa stone," I blurted out, gasping for air. Gerry shot back at me, "It's men's business."

My mind raced, looking for something to say. Gerry was still looking into my eyes. They were warm, yet they seemed to search for something inside me. For what seemed like an eternity, I was unable to reply. My eyes kept darting about the room. Finally, I gathered my wits and tried to speak calmly, "Yes, but you see the stone has never been unwrapped while in my care, I hold it in great respect. I use the stone in my work as a medium, and uh ... the voice that comes to me with the help of the stone is a male voice."

Gerry leaned back and laughed, "Well that's good."

We all laughed and the atmosphere became light again. He slipped the pink crystal back into his pocket. I could not resist, "Would you like to see the stone?" There was fear in Gerry's eyes as he declined the invitation.

My brain went blank. I wasn't quite sure what to do. Gee, I should be halfway down the hallway by now, bringing the stone to the kitchen. I had to say something. "Speaking of stones uh, you know at the last spring equinox, I visited the giant mystery rock Uluru. I really loved the place, and I agree with the Koori that it is sacred. I chose not to walk on the rock out of respect for the Aboriginal people."

Then I described how Alcheringa had presented himself through me at the rock.

Gerry's eyebrows shot up. He leaned forward, "One of my Koori friends has an unseen being who speaks through him, calling himself Alcheringa."

In that tiny moment, I felt as one with the Koori, my credentials had been established.

Then, Gerry gave me the strangest look, "Do you know of the hieroglyphs at Kariong, near Gosford?"

"Yes, I've heard about those, I'm told they're Aboriginal," I replied.

"I've been there many times, and the hieroglyphs are not Aboriginal. I would like to take you there to see them. Do you think that Alcheringa might talk to me if we go there?"

I said, "Yes" without even thinking about it.

Suddenly I felt as if I was going to be initiated. Alcheringa had told me over a year ago that he would one day speak through me to an Aborigine.

We went to Kariong the following week.

It was a very special day, the tenth day of the tenth month. My friend Karen joined us. She overheard me talking about the trip, and insisted that she go with us. It seemed like a good idea. We arrived in the late afternoon after a four-hour drive.

Walking ahead of us in the bush, Gerry occasionally threw small stones to inform the spirits that we were coming, so as not to surprise them. He told us it would be icy cold at the site, but for me the weather felt quite pleasant.

Gerry instructed us to eat some of the tips of the young leaves of the gum tree to become 'one' with the landscape. Then he asked the spirits and elementals for permission to enter their area. As for our contribution, Karen brought a video camera and I had my 35mm still camera. Well, we are hi-tech white girls, what can I say?

We climbed towards a huge rock that seemed to have broken free from the mountain to form a narrow chasm with a flat floor. The back third was roofed in by a large flat rock. As we crawled through a tiny opening into the chasm, I was stunned by the images that lay before us. The rock walls were covered in breathtaking hieroglyphs. Karen and I were amazed. There were hundreds of them. The chasm was a time capsule carved in stone.

Many of them looked Egyptian. I'm no expert, but I clearly recognized a carving of the Egyptian god Anubis. Others looked like symbols or pictographs of some event.

Moving to one of the walls, I gently touched several of the hieroglyphs. My fingers tingled as they ran over the ancient images.

Some of them seemed to evoke distant emotions that I couldn't quite place. As I began to take photographs, I noticed that many of them were very clear and deeply cut. Then I said, "These were cut into the stone by a laser rod."

How could I have known that?

Karen was busy videotaping with her camera. In the centre of the chasm, Gerry stood with his eyes closed, as if in deep meditation. Then Karen let out a small gasp. I turned to see her pointing intently at a glyph of a pregnant woman.

I felt a sense of detachment.

Gerry seemed to sense the change, and led us to the top of a rock overlooking the chasm. We sat facing each other. Karen started her video camera as Alcheringa began to speak through me.

"Greetings my friends, I am Alcheringa. I have waited a long time for this meeting to take place. It is my pleasure to be here. I have known each of you many lifetimes before; you see we are all connected to the worlds of the stars.

"Many are curious about the drawings carved upon this rock. Each of you has a feeling that they were cut by beings from another world. Indeed, many of them were. For millions of years, beings of other worlds, other stars, even other galaxies have visited the little Earth. Many have influenced the genetic evolvement of living creatures on the Earth such as fish, land animals, and insects. It is a living planet with life forces in every part of it. But then, you are aware of this.

"There are many things to speak of, but this is not the time. Much of the information will unfold gradually, for we have a greater plan. Each part will come together so that a larger picture will be recognized and understood by those who live on the planet Earth.

"There is a great need for all on this planet to understand the mother that you call Earth, the mother who looks after you and nourishes everything that lives upon her. There is a need to love and respect the mother Earth, to nurture her. I know that each of you understands this deep within, and will help us to spread that understanding. One of you has a question."

Gerry spoke up, "Is there anything else we should know about this site, does it need protection?"

"This place has been protected all along. We will continue this protection until it is time to come forth in a public way.

This ancient place holds keys to a larger picture. These images will unite, open up, and evolve many who will remember. The time now is too soon, it will happen in a time not far ahead."

Gerry asked, "Is there anything you want us to do?"

"In actual fact my son, you are already following our inspiration. You have allowed yourself to guide these people. Not just at this meeting place today. We desired this to take place. There will be many times when you realise that unseen hands are at work. There is nothing for you to worry about, we know that you are willing to be of service.

"Be aware my son, keep yourself alert. Deal with each problem as it is put before you. Many work with you and give assistance. We will sometimes push you a little further than what you are used to. This is done knowing that you have the ability to work from that point.

"As each of you takes a step in life, know that we are with you. We come from the world of light. We come to you with love, from a point of God. We ask that you be not afraid.

"We come to assist, and are ready whenever you call upon us. In some way, help will always be given to you. There is really nothing more to say at this time other than to keep up the good work. I will take my leave now. I thank you for welcoming me here. It is no coincidence that we are all here today. More will evolve very soon as you shall see. God bless you all."

Alcheringa's presence departed, yet I still felt a warm energy around me.

Gerry stood up and asked us to follow him. We walked further up the mountain to Whale Rock, a site that overlooked the Brisbane waters and Broken Bay beyond. This was a large flat rock with distinct cobblestone markings cut into it. As we walked onto the rock, both Karen and I lowered our heads.

Each of us had the distinctive feeling that we were walking under something. We looked up in unison. There was nothing of course, just our over-active imaginations, or was it? Karen and I had both experienced identical reactions to this location. My heart began to beat faster.

The Birthing Canal

Gerry said he had been to this place many times, using it as a healing rock. He motioned to the area around the rock, telling us that Aboriginal families used to live here, eating their meals at the exact spot where we were standing. To one side of us was the men's business site, to the other, the women's business site. He showed us a part of the rock where a formation had been gouged out, like a cradle. Gerry told us that in the old times, Aboriginal women had used it as a birthing canal.

Karen decided to lie in the rock cradle. Moments later, she appeared to go to sleep. Then her eyes began to move as if she were in REM sleep, a dream state. I watched her curiously, for what seemed like minutes. Then she sat upright with her eyes opened wide.

"What did you feel?" I asked.

Karen look confused, "The ecstasy of childbirth. At the same time I was also feeling abandoned, and yet I knew I was there with others."

Gerry moved close to Karen and looked at her intently with eyes that were suddenly huge, "What about the baby?"

Karen seemed stunned by his question.

"I... I don't really know," she replied in a voice that wavered.

Here I began to feel a kind of detachment from reality again, similar to what I feel before I communicate with Alcheringa, but different.

Gerry walked to the edge of the rock overlooking Broken Bay. It was just starting to get dark and twinkling lights were beginning to appear in the town below. He turned and motioned for me to come closer to the edge, then pointed towards the water. There was a dreamy look in his eyes.

"See where that little boat is down in the middle of the water, I think that is where the ship went down. Just focus on it Valerie."

A rush came over me. I felt my hands reaching out towards the water and was suddenly overcome. A sense of deep sadness wrenched my whole body. I could hear the sounds of terror, there was crying and wailing. I had to release the pain, the fright, and the overwhelming sense of loss that was overtaking me.

Suddenly it was broad daylight. The land looked different than it does now, more tropical and dense. It was extremely hot and I was having trouble breathing. The air was thick and liquid, as if I were breathing under water. Each breath was painful.

My outstretched arms were long and thin. The skin on them was a blue white colour, almost transparent. My head felt elongated.

I experienced an overwhelming feeling of total disbelief. My husband, children, and many friends had all been killed. How could this have happened? The feeling of disbelief was replaced by a sense of betrayal. Then came the rising of anger, an emotional experience that the person I was experiencing had never known before.

I recoiled from the impact of her anger back into what I thought was normal reality. Beside me, Karen and Gerry were gasping and on the edge of crying. We appeared to be sharing some kind of group experience. Whale Rock seemed to be in another time.

Then the veil was torn away and the memories began to rush in. We had all come in peace from Pleiades/Lyra, and another place before that sounded like Altaah. I collapsed to my knees as the white-hot daylight and choking atmosphere returned.

There had been a desperate attempt to get away from something. We had come in peace on a mission of God and were attacked by those who were not of the light of love. Far below, a saucer-like starship lay broken in the waters of the bay. The occupants of the ship were badly injured and traumatised. Their fear and pain echoed into my mind as if I were sharing their consciousness. Dolphins appeared, reacting to their unspoken pleas for help, pushing some of them ashore.

Another saucer-ship, the one on which I had arrived, hovered over the crippled saucer picking up survivors in the water.

Those already on the shore, exposed to the searing light of the sun above, screamed in pain as they sought cover from the intense radiation. Some had sustained terrible injuries, the agony of which I was directly sharing.

My senses reeled and I turned my head away. Others stood behind me, viewing the scene with the same horror. They were all aliens, not of this Earth. I looked down at my arms and body. My God, I was one of them.

I looked up to see Eleura amongst the group, remembering her face and name as if I had known her for centuries. Her large black eyes looked back at me and I connected with her experience. Her husband Ujeshet was pinned by a metal beam to the control console of the saucer-ship lying in the water below. He was taking a long time to die under the waters of an ocean he had never known before. Eleura carried his unborn child, and was conveying the consciousness of the tiny being to Ujeshet as he asked her, "What about the baby?"

I sought out the consciousness of Ujeshet and connected with him, sending my love and concern. As my husband's brother radiated his love back to me there was a loud pop, and I was back in the twilight air of Whale Rock staring directly into the eyes of Gerry Bostock.

For a brief instant, Gerry and I connected by mind, just as I had with Ujeshet. Yes, that was it. Gerry was Ujeshet in that distant time. I turned to Karen and had the same connection. Karen was Eleura.

We looked at each other and realized why we had come to this place. We had come back to remember, this was the time.

We reached out to each other and moved into a tight embrace of reunion. Old friends had come back to live out lives on Earth for this moment in time.

The twilight air was icy cold, yet I felt washed in the warm love of God that was around us and in us. I felt eternally blessed as the three of us joined hand to wrist to form two triangles, one above the other, in an ancient form of greeting, the source of the Star of David.

We raised our interlocked arms out to the stars in thanksgiving. Far above, the soft light of the Pleiades shone down upon us, caressing our faces and drying our tears like a loving mother who had found her long lost children at last. In the exquisite moment of that soothing embrace, we were healed.

Helen Vincent (Karen in this book) on the left;
Valerie Barrow, centre; Gerry Bostock on the right

CHAPTER 2

Alcheringa Tells of the Mission of the Starship Rexegena
Pamela Goddard's Regression

It seemed as if we raced through the fading twilight back to the car. Now we were three people with a very different relationship than we had just moments before. My whole life had suddenly changed. Huge questions posed themselves in my mind. What had just happened on that rock? Who was I when I experienced being that alien person? Who and what am I now?

The first part of the journey back home was in silence, each of us involved in our own thoughts about what had happened. Karen looked troubled and seemed to be making an effort to hold back from crying. Gerry finally broke the ice.

"When I was sixteen I had a particularly vivid dream. I thought about it for many days afterward because it seemed so real at the time. There was a certain dynamic about it that made me feel as if it had actually happened.

"In the dream, I was on-board a huge space craft in orbit around a blue and green planet. Everything on the ship had a bright sheen to it, particularly the uniforms of the people. There was lots of hurried activity, coloured lights were flashing, and bells were ringing.

"Everyone was in a hurry following certain procedures, as if there were an emergency. I was seeing everything through the eyes of a crew member, perhaps a pilot or navigator. I felt an urgency to get my family together before some imminent event occurred.

"The scene changed, and I was on-board a smaller craft escaping from the mother ship. As I looked out the porthole, I became aware of two things, the planet we were heading towards, and the mothership we were leaving. The mothership was an immense saucer or mushroom-shaped silvery craft with hundreds of smaller ships leaving it, one of them containing my wife. They were all heading away in every direction, trying to escape as quickly as possible. Suddenly there was a blinding flash and the mother ship blew up. The impact on me was so overwhelming that I woke from the dream.

"Tonight on Whale rock, I re-lived that dream on the small ship as it hurtled towards the planet. My craft had been crippled in an explosion, and I was frantically trying to get it under control. The planet was rushing towards us very fast. As we broke through the cloud layer, I saw the surface below, all green and blue, so beautiful in contrast to the fear that filled my heart. I saw a small bay filled with bright blue water, and struggled to focus my mind on bringing the ship to a gentle landing on the shore.

"I sensed the ship trying to respond, but it could not slow quickly enough. We struck the water hard. I could feel the bulkhead behind me collapse and pin my body to the control panel.

"The ship began to fill with water through the huge hole that was torn in its side. I signalled for everyone to get out. Several people tried to free me from the control panel, but the water pushed them away. As the ship turned on its side and sank, I tasted the salty water of a strange ocean. All I could think about was my wife and unborn child."

Karen's face seemed both beautiful and sad as she looked at him, "I was your wife."

Gerry turned to her, "Yes, and you gave me such comfort in that moment, bringing me the consciousness of the child that was within you. You gave me hope that our kind would survive in that strange and beautiful world. Our love was so strong, you were with me every moment during the four days it took for me to die. Our bodies were different then, charged with so much energy. But our people could not get to me in time, and so I passed on."

Karen's eyes filled with tears, "Three days after your death I gave birth to our child, lying in the cradle of rock that was cut for me by the laser rod. He was the first of our people born on the Earth. We called him **P'taah** of the rock. He fought so hard to live. We all worked to save him. The poor child could not breathe the air. We were all choking on the thick damp gas of the planet. When he died, we all knew that we would have to struggle to survive as a people in that beautiful but deadly place."

I had to stop the car; I couldn't see the road anymore. We all got out to take a breath in the cool night air. The sense of betrayal and anger I felt earlier began to rise within me again. I turned to Gerry and Karen, "What is going on here? Who are we and why this happening to us?

Karen stabbed her finger at me, "Who are you?"

I snapped back, "I am Egarina, the communicator. My husband is the commander-in-chief of the Star Ship Rex-egena. We have come in peace on a mission from God to take this planet back from the Reptoids. They are not of the light and must leave!" I stopped, gasping for breath.

Where did those words come from?

Karen looked at me quizzically, "What's a Reptoid?"

I felt detached from reality again, like I was back at Kariong. I sat on a nearby rock and sighed, "Damned if I know."

Gerry seemed to understand what was happening, "All of us must have been together before in some other life, but we were not human, at least not human as we know it. Now we have come back together to remember, which we are definitely doing. All we can do is continue to remember and see what happens. I have the feeling that you are some kind of messenger Valerie, and that we are here to help you."

I looked at him with a frown, "Why do you think that?"

"A **Churinga** is a message stick, or stone used by the Aborigine to send word from one tribe to another. Alcheringa means messenger, as in the one who carries the stick or stone. You have the Alcheringa stone. Even your home has that name. That is why I first came to see you."

"But why me?" I replied weakly.

"You just told us why, you are the communicator." There would be no sleep that night.

Six AM, I lay in bed staring at the ceiling. In my mind, I ran over and over the events of the previous day, trying to understand what had happened. It was real, not some imaginary event. I shared it with two others who confirmed it. Each time I thought about it, something new would come in. I was spontaneously remembering little fragments of a distant past.

I got up from the bed and put on my robe. In my study, I lifted the Alcheringa stone from its box. I sat cross-legged on the floor holding the stone and tried to still my thoughts. Softly I called the name Alcheringa, and then felt the familiar sense of detachment.

"It is I, Alcheringa. How may I help you my child?"

The question had burned in my mind all night, "What was the mission of the Rexegena in coming to Earth?"

"The mission. Ah yes, the mission! Very good dear one, you proceed quite quickly, just as we had hoped.

"This was a very exciting project in the star worlds at that time. We looked forward to achieving what the hierarchy had set before us. The mission was to take many volunteers on a massive living starship to the planet Mu, as we called the Earth in those days. The idea was to set up a base so that a new race could be established, a race that came with the energy of love, harmony, and good will to all. This new energy was to influence what was already taking place on Mu.

"An aspect of myself had been appointed commander in chief. It was quite a responsibility, but I loved the challenge. My wife, who in that life was you, and our four children, accompanied me. You were all very willing to join me in that journey."

My eyebrows crept up, "I was your wife?"

"Yes, and I loved you dearly, I do so even now. Let us continue. The Rexegena set off from the eighth star of the Pleiadean group with fifty thousand on board. We were going to a place we had never been before. The fifty thousand were from various places within this galaxy. Everyone mingled well together, and all were interested in knowing one another. There was a tremendous sense of excitement and expectation.

"The corner of the galaxy into which we were heading was occupied by races that were not of the same belief patterns as we. Different belief patterns exist in the star worlds, just as they do on your Earth. Our mission was to change those belief patterns, not with force, but with the influence of love energy, so that these people would come to experience the crystal light. Then these races would understand and know compassion, and how it feels to interact with those of love, light, and joy.

"Now we must travel back to an earlier time so that you will understand what took place.

"Billions of years before, the Earth itself had come into development, a place that would be suitable for occupation by the hierarchy of which we had come. In those early days, the planet's surface was flat and lifeless. We planned the Earth to become a Garden of Eden. The word Eden comes from a sound which breaks through the molecule and the atom, helping to create the form.

"The plan required the crust of the Earth to change its shape. Comets and meteors were allowed to hit the surface so that there was created an up and down. Eventually, there was an exchange of gases and water was introduced onto the planet. With the water, forms of life could be introduced that would be nurtured.

"The hierarchy sent things to create life and help it multiply. Many things were planted in the early stages of the Earth's development. We sent spores and other life forms that could grow and develop on the planet. The changes taking place on the Earth actually fired these elements and substances to create various living forms. The hierarchy created a grid around the planet to help stabilize it, allowing more growth to take place.

"Little forms of life such as fungus, molluscs, and others of low development began to grow and multiply. Many from the hierarchy and the angelic realms worked together to help this take place.

"It was at this time there was interest shown by many of the cultures throughout the cosmos, in particular the extra-terrestrial beings that already existed in this corner of the galaxy. They began coming and going to the Earth, showing much interest in the place.

"These beings came to Earth many millions of years before the journey of the Rexegena. They were created by a different hierarchy, one that came more from the point of self and power. While the energies in these beings were of the light, they did not possess the energy of love and compassion.

"They were the **Reptoids**, and as their name suggests, they were reptilian. We say once again, while they understood the light and had the intelligence that goes with it, they did not understand love. They did not have that created within them in the first place.

"There were other races created as such in this corner of the galaxy, including the **Dinoid**, who also came to the Earth. Because of the missing element of love, dissension eventually arose among them. This resulted in competition and even wars. This was not unusual, it happened in many places in the universe during those early times hundreds of millions of years ago. You must understand that these races had been created by others who had turned away from the light of The One.

"Those of the angelic realms who had been working to create this Garden of Eden came from the **Elohim**. Some were caught up with what was taking place on this Earth, and were concerned about the visitations by the Reptoid and Dinoid races, which were starting to claim the planet for themselves.

"The Reptoids and the Dinoids were also beginning to create many life forms themselves on the planet Earth. They created through genetic engineering, for they were very good at it and enjoyed it immensely.

"While the Reptoids and Dinoids were actually different races, there was a similarity in their nature that allowed them to live in a sort of uneasy way together on the Earth. They both had abilities in genetic engineering and between them created many different life forms. Look at the face of almost any frog in your time and you will see the natural face of the Dinoid.

"The two races began to work together and started creating, almost like an artist's brush, many different life forms. It became a sort of competition to see who could out do the other, for they rather enjoyed this.

"The dinosaur was created by them. This was a Dinoid as well as Reptoid influence, although the dinosaur bore the name of the Dinoid. Through creative competition between the two races, the dinosaurs became larger and more ferocious. As they became larger, they became full of teeth and very dangerous. The animals continued to breed with one another, and the numbers increased dramatically. The foliage was being eaten very quickly, and in many places the Earth became desert like. Waste materials from the creatures and their dead bodies littered the landscape.

"A way was needed to have these materials fall back into the Earth, so the Reptoids and Dinoids created virus, bacteria, and parasite forms to assist this process in taking place.

"Many millions of years passed with all this activity on Earth. Other visitors came from different star worlds to visit. They did not stay for very long because of the danger that filled the place. The Earth had become overrun by Reptoid and Dinoid creations.

"This did not fit with the plan of the Elohim, and there were some who sought to try and take it back. This was more difficult than first thought, so the Elohim decided to monitor what was taking place on the Earth. They sent beings who changed their form and entered the waters to become what you know as the whale. In this form, they were the first and only mammal upon the Earth. In fact, they were the only mammal for a very long time.

"The whales were able to hold the light and the plan within their consciousness. They helped the Elohim to continue their work and influence upon this planet, even though the Reptoid and Dinoid races were busily going about their own plans.

"The form of the whale, operating in the waters, did not interfere with what was taking place with the Reptoids and Dinoids on the land. They all lived in reasonable harmony. The Reptoids and Dinoids were not aware that the Elohim were allowing it to take place. There was an unwritten agreement allowing two developments on the Earth at the same time.

"There was a greater plan, one that this planet could be used as a base by people who came with love and light to influence those in this corner of the galaxy where there was so much darkness. Events were scheduled that would change all of this, events that would eventually allow the Rexegena to set off on its great mission."

"When did the Rexegena come to Earth?" I asked.

"That would have been just over nine hundred thousand years ago."

"Nine hundred thousand years ago, that's a long time." I noted.

"Not in the star worlds. Someone is coming to see you. There are some things we want you to do."

"But I'm not expecting anybody," I said, as the phone rang. I answered to hear a woman's voice.

"Valerie, my name is Pamela Goddard. I came to see you about a year ago. You may not remember me, but I'm getting very strong messages to call you and I don't know why."

"Um, yes, I remember you," I replied somewhat thunder-struck. Pulling out my address book, I found her name. Next to it, I had written *clar*. Pamela was a clairvoyant. My mouth automatically said, "Well, perhaps we should get together sometime and talk."

"Oh good," she replied, "I can be at your place at two o'clock, sound okay?"

"Uh, sure why not, see you here at two." I hung up the phone, "Is Pamela Goddard the one, Alcheringa?"

"Yes, that's the one."

Pamela's car came up the driveway at exactly two o'clock. My eye caught the wall clock in the kitchen and I noted her promptness. As the second-hand swept past twelve, the phone rang. The caller was my friend Rachel. I had been struggling to help Rachel through a crisis. She was either getting a little carried away with psychic experiences or there was something very wrong with her.

The doorbell rang. I recognized Pamela immediately and invited her to have a seat on the lounge while I finished my phone call.

I returned to the phone to hear Rachel talking as if I had never left. Rachel was confused and unsure of herself. She felt that the two of us might have a 'karmic' thing together. She wanted to meet with me and 'work it out'. I stammered that I had a guest who had just arrived, and promised to call her back later.

An instant headache settled over me, I felt depressed. Apologizing for my mood, I offered Pamela hot lemon tea. As we did the little ceremony, Pamela tried to calm my nerves.

"I understand just how you feel. I have an acquaintance I'm trying to help who is doing the same thing to me. She has some 'special' things she has to do, and at the same time, she feels unsure of herself and needs constant assurance that she is on the right path. On top of that, Rachel is ..."

"Rachel?" I interrupted.

"That's right," Pamela replied, "Rachel is ..."

My eyes narrowed, "Rachel O'Meara?"

The tiniest fraction of Pamela's composure slipped as she let out a small gasp. We stared at each other in silence for a magical second before breaking into laughter.

Pamela shrugged her shoulders and sipped her tea, "Okay Valerie, I'm here, what do you want with me?"

We laughed a bit more as I looked at the package of pictures from Kariong sticking out of my purse, the ones I had rushed to the shop that morning to have developed. "Well, let's see," I said.

I moved to the bookshelf, picked up the Alcheringa stone, and walked over to Pamela in one smooth movement, "Do you mind if I set this in your lap?" I sat it on her lap before she had a chance to answer.

She looked at it a bit askance, "No, I guess not. What is it?"

I took the pictures from my purse. "It's a stone."

Pamela eyed it a bit closer, "Oh, what's that stuff covering it?"

Sitting back in my chair, I removed the photos from the envelope, "It's the bark of the paper bark tree." Pamela touched the bark to examine the texture, "It's, so..."

"Aboriginal," I interjected, "Would you please look at these pictures?"

Pamela took the photos.

The phone rang again. It was Karen and she was unhappy.

"This is terrible, I looked at the video, and everything on it is all jerky. I can't make any of the hieroglyphs out. We have to go back to Kariong."

Pamela gave the photos a cursory glance, "Hmm, these rock carvings look Egyptian."

"Go back, what do you mean by jerky?" I asked.

Pamela continued, "This one is Anubis, the god of the underworld I think."

Karen continued to complain, "You know, the picture bounces back and forth between glyphs. It only stops for a second and then bounces away again. I can't see a thing."

"Didn't you take that video Karen?"

"I've always wanted to go to Egypt," said Pamela.

"Of course I did Valerie, I know that. You never touched my camera. It doesn't matter. They're no good anyway, we have to go back."

"When did you go there?" inquired Pamela.

I pulled the phone away from my ear and looked at Pamela, "Those were taken at Kariong yesterday."

"Kariong?"

"Yes, near Gosford, about four hours from here." I returned to the phone, "You can look at my pictures Karen, they're all nice and sharp."

My husband walked in and introduced himself to Pamela.

Karen seemed to calm down, "Oh, well I'm coming over right now to look at them."

"Karen, I can't see you right now, I'm in a meeting. How about tomorrow?"

"Tomorrow? Well in that case we should just go back to Kariong."

"Do you seriously want to go back to Kariong?"

"Yes."

My husband turned and looked at me in amazement, "Are you really going back to Kariong?"

Pamela smiled, "Oh, can I go with you?"

Things got fuzzy for a moment, John was never interested in Kariong before, "Well, okay if you like."

John shrugged his shoulders and walked out.

Karen was delighted, "Fantastic, I'll be there at five AM, we should get an early start. Bye."

"What?" I replied. Karen hung up. It all just happened so quickly.

Pamela looked curiously at the photos, "These sure look real to me."

I sat next to her, "They're real Pamela. Look at the pictures carefully, see if there is anything in them that you recognize or get a feeling from."

Pamela began a closer inspection of the pictures. At first, she had no reaction, flipping through them slowly, regarding each one calmly. She stopped at one, held it closer, and stared at one of the rock carvings. Pamela's face began to change, her calm demeanour falling away as a tear tumbled down her cheek onto the picture. She closed her eyes and a look of horror came over her face.

"Oh no, I don't want to remember this, there was too much suffering."

"It's okay," I replied. Taking the pictures, I wiped the teardrop away and looked closely at the frame she was staring at. "Pamela, what did you see when you closed your eyes?"

"The ship, I saw the ship, the same one I see in my dreams. It's always that ship, the one that brought me here. It was so big and solid, how could they have destroyed it?" She began to cry. A memory in Pamela was being triggered by one of the pictures.

"Pamela, I have those memories too, and I know others who do as well." Pamela wiped her eyes with her hands, "What is happening to me?"

"I'm not quite sure. You're the first person I've shown these photos to. I remembered the ship at Kariong along with two others. All we know is that these rock carvings are some kind of message that seems to awaken memories."

Pamela allowed me to slowly lead her back to that memory. In a manner that ranged from panicky and desperate to calm and lucid, she let out the pent up emotions of the ship in her dreams.

"I'm stuck here on this planet. We have nothing and can barely breathe the air. I only came here because my family wanted to come, and now they are all dead. What am I doing in this terrible place?

"I have to help the injured ones. There is no time to suffer the loss of my husband and children. I have fifty things to do, and everyone is going crazy. How could this have happened?

"We are devastated, except for our emergency rations there is no food. We don't know what we can eat on this planet. Even the water is dangerous, filled with tiny creatures we have never seen before.

"I am exhausted, working day and night. Everyone is asking me questions because I have the knowledge of healing.

"Now it's evening and I am down by the water. We can come out in the open when the sun is down. I'm walking along by myself feeling a bit tattered. There is work all the time, healing bodies and putting them together again."

I asked her to describe herself.

"I'm quite tall, willowy I would say. I don't think I have hair. I have big eyes. My skin is very smooth, pale and transparent, kind of whitish, greyish, blue."

"What about your head?" I asked.

"It feels long, kind of flat on the back. Oh, I still have my laboratory cap on. Ah, I do have some hair, it's bunched up under my cap. Hmm, the cap feels just like skin."

"What do you do in the laboratory?" I asked.

"I'm there with the test tubes and bottles, nothing too fancy because we have a shortage of them. In the beginning, we had what seemed like a first aid kit, now we have a sort of laboratory. We are matching genes for inter-breeding."

"Inter-breeding? What are you inter-breeding with?"

"We are inter-breeding with the upstanding ape-looking creatures from this planet. Everything must be done quickly. Otherwise, the new race will be lost. That's what we came here to do, so it must be done. Things will not keep in this atmosphere – we have no working refrigeration. It's all so new to us."

"Wait, with ape creatures? How are you doing this inter-breeding?"

"I am one of the volunteers who will be artificially inseminated. Many of the other women have volunteered. We are the ones who will carry the new race into being, a race that can survive in this place."

"But why are you doing this with ape creatures from the Earth, was this the original plan?"

"No, but we cannot survive here as we are, our newborn children die. It is very difficult. Everything has to be very precise. I still have trouble with breathing.

"I have learned a lot from a Reptoid who joined us. He is very helpful and honest, completely turned around in his ways. I like him very much and can feel his humour. He has shown us how to use vegetation for food and medicine."

"But what happens with this inter-breeding thing with the apes?"

"Some women give birth one after another. This goes on for a while. The women give birth very easily as no pain is involved. The children are very well looked after. Later, they begin to breed amongst themselves."

I must admit that I was in a state of shock. Here were survivors from a star ship, cast onto the Earth, attempting genetic engineering from a first aid kit, "Does the inter-breeding with these apes succeed?"

"Some of them don't turn out quite right, some of them do. There is still much genetic engineering work going on to match the people."

I gasped, "What do you mean some of them don't turn out quite right ?"

"It is all for a good purpose. The whole idea is to bring love, light, and peace to the Earth, so that people don't make judgments of others, so that we don't get caught up with wars, hostility, and anger.

"I am old now. I have all this research and knowledge inside of me. I do a lot of teaching to the new ones. I teach about my work with plant life. It seems I know an awful lot of things.

"The first part of my life was secure, I had a good family. Then I was stranded here and I lost everyone. I never saw my home world again. I can feel that loss now, it's terrible. I pushed it all down inside of me, so very deep.

"This influenced all my other lives, and it explains my lives of solitude. I've had so many just on my own. Rather than face the hurt and pain, I have lived my life as a nun, or lived by myself. It's all because of the fear of letting my emotions go. Now I have gone and done it again in this life."

Pamela opened her eyes and the tears began to fall anew. "Isn't that interesting?" She put her head on my shoulder and cried.

CHAPTER 3

Valerie goes to Kariong with
John and Karen
John Barrow's Regression

The rain pounded against the roof of our car. Kariong could have been a million miles away at that moment, yet was just outside. We looked out our windows at the grey sky, lost in thought.

Pamela, the one I had really agreed to come for, was not with us. After finishing her emotional release, a peace descended over her. At the end, she looked at me, smiling.

"We were so different then, we had so much love. We ran on love. We pulled our weight and trained the new children. Even when their abilities and brain power turned out to be different than ours, we continued to work with them. We did it because they were born with spiritual understanding and they had the light of love within them. We did what we came to do. Don't you see? We succeeded in bringing light to this place. At that time, it was all that mattered."

She leaned close to me, "You're going to meet more people. You have to. They too are going to feel the dream. Like me, they will need to talk to you. How can they not? The work you do, you must keep going. You have to attract them. Everyone has come back and is here now. You must bring them together to help others with the changes in the Earth that are coming."

What do I have to do with changes in the Earth?

I have to walk very carefully, so that what I am given I don't pre-empt with imagination, or with what I want things to be. There is a need to be strict with myself, to stay with just what is given, to not try to understand until more is given. Only then will a full understanding be realised.

Karen arrived on time and we all climbed into the car. I looked at John. He was not happy and stared back at me to prove the point. After Pamela had left, I asked him why he suddenly wanted to go to Kariong.

He shot back, "Kariong, what makes you think I want to go to Kariong?"

"But you said ..."

"I asked if you were going back to Kariong because I couldn't believe you would drive all that way again after just one day."

So, I persuaded him to come anyway, but he was not keen on the idea. He viewed the grey skies with an annoyed expression.

"That will be enough rain, thank you."

I obligingly rolled down the window and repeated his request. Two minutes later, the sun peeked out from behind a cloud and the rain stopped. I will never be able to explain that one.

We emerged from the car and looked around. The day was fabulous, the cool air scrubbed fresh and new. Flowers appeared everywhere as if to welcome us, the raindrops on them sparkling in the bright sun. In the sky above us, three rainbows spread their marvellous colours. Two eagles appeared and soared back and forth through them. These were very good signs. We began to walk up the hill.

Karen, repeating what Gerry had shown us, pulled off some of the young leaf tips of a gum tree and nibbled them to connect with the energy of the area. She offered some to John and me.

John muttered, "No thanks, but if you find some hot fish and chips let me know."

I ignored his shallow attempt at humour and asked aloud for permission to enter the area, then stuffed the leaf tips into my mouth.

We climbed the hill to the hieroglyphs.

Seeing them for the second time, they seemed to make more sense. The glyph of a pregnant woman seemed to connect to Karen, and again she was drawn to it. Other glyphs showed people who appeared to be laid out as if they had died or were injured. I viewed a glyph that could have been a star ship, with many smaller ships shooting out from it. One was upside down under a wavy line. Was that the one that went into the water? There was a drawing of a bell. Was that the one that sounded so urgently when we had to abandon the ship?

John eyed them coolly, noting how clear and new some of them looked, too new to be ancient.

I replied, "I don't question that some of them look new, but some of them look very old. I believe some of them are ancient, written by a past race."

John shrugged his shoulders, "Well I don't know about that. It does seem familiar though, as if I had dreamt about the place. Maybe I should check it out."

After a few moments, he began to inspect around the perimeter of the site, almost as if on patrol, searching for invaders. Why did I feel I had to defend the hieroglyphs?

Karen sat cross-legged on a rock staring at the carving of the pregnant woman. Beside her on a rigid tripod, her video camera shot a long steady close-up. Karen can really do things right when she wants to.

John suddenly yelled, then ran off down the hill. I walked out to the edge to see him running towards a group of long haired teenagers who were racing their cars up and down the dirt trail and doing *wheelies*. Two young girls leaned up against our car watching them.

John encountered the group and started waving his hands. He was too far away for me to hear. Then he pulled out his mobile phone and started to dial it. I could hear myself saying, "Oh no," as I watched him. Then the kids gave in and moved off down the road.

After a sigh of relief, I returned to the hieroglyphs. Above me, Karen had moved to Whale rock and was looking at the birthing cradle cut from the rock. Once again, she lay in the cut out hollow. John returned to the hieroglyphs, breathing hard and limping. He sat next to me.

"Everything okay?" I asked.

"All secure," he replied, catching his breath. Then he looked at the hieroglyphs that were all around us, for a few moments.

"I've been here twice you know."

"I don't remember you being here twice."

"Yes, I was here once before with you."

For a second I thought he could be right, but then again I knew this was his first visit. I turned to him, "Tell me about the first visit."

"There, that one."

John raised his hand and pointed at one of the glyphs on the chasm wall,

I walked to the wall and pointed at an Egyptian looking figure with an animal head, "This one?"

"Yes," he replied, "the one wearing the space helmet."

A smile broke out on my face as I realised that John was playing a little joke on me; he does that sometimes. Looking at the figure, I thought that the little line drawn around his head could be regarded as a space helmet. So, I decided to go for it, "Why is he wearing a space helmet?"

John viewed me firmly, "They didn't like the air here, so they wore them. That's one of the Cat people who came here with me."

I snickered loudly and asked, "The what?"

"The Cat people. I was in charge of the mission, I should know. We came here to sort out those Reptoids."

My smile vanished. John said the word Reptoid, and I hadn't told him about the Reptoids yet. John was not joking. This conversation was not the kind I would normally be having with him.

Let me just interject here. One of the many reasons I love John is because he supports my work, not on a line item basis, but in a philosophical sense that I dearly appreciate. Yet, he is about as New Age as the internal combustion engine. An ex-military, suit and tie kind of business entrepreneur guy, John is, well ... he's straight. So, you can see how I am in a little bit of a quandary here.

I sat down next to him and thought to myself, *Okay Valerie, you did this with Pamela yesterday and it worked. Let's give it a go on John, he can always deny it later.*

"Tell me about the Cat people."

John frowned and leaned back against a rock, gesturing dramatically, "Most of the time they think they are right."

I chuckled, "So that would be a Leonine trait huh? Did you say you were on a mission somewhere?"

John became agitated, "We are going somewhere, but I feel in limbo. I don't know where we have come from or where we are going to."

"That's okay," I assured him, "just relax, allow yourself to go deeper into the memory. Do you know why you are so aggressive, are the others aggressive also?"

"They are like lions, they have huge lion energy. These half man and half animal bipeds come from different planets. I've always thought that cats and dogs come from a different dimension."

"Are there biped beings that look like dogs?" I asked.

"Yes, but they are lesser beings. You only have to look at the cat family to see that they are superior to everybody else, or so they think they are. Even domestic cats believe they are in charge, at least from their standpoint, whereas dogs are servile generally speaking."

I had no idea where this was going. Nothing except the Reptoid word seemed to fit. I asked him to move on his memory to when he arrived.

"Of course. Before me are the controls of the ship. They are crystal, pyramid shaped, with light around them. They steer the ship, but I have no idea how.

"As I look out the window, I see deep black space filled with stars. Arrayed around me is what is definitely an attacking force.

"I am aware of these reptiles below. These beings also have a high intelligence and technology. They are suppressing other beings and that is why we are here, to sort them out."

Now we were on track, "Who are the Reptoids suppressing?"

"The Reptoids have created a very bad situation here on Earth. Our mission is to go and fix them, to wipe them out if need be. The other ones that they are suppressing are, well I don't know, other kinds of creatures that have come from ..."

John wavered for a moment, then looked at me intently.

"If we have to, we will use our technology to annihilate these reptiles because they are causing far too much trouble. They're not just on one planet you know, there are other places where they have created their dinosaurs. They all have to be brought to heel.

"We have the power to direct meteors, that is like our artillery, our bombers. We have laser beams you could equate to infantry. These beams can petrify the Reptoids into fossil instantly, or any other creature for that matter.

"The command ships in this peace corps are very small. The actual workhorses, the meteors and the planetoids, are huge. We are a highly developed force. We come here to police, but if we have to attack, we are deadly. We can blow stuff away. We have the technology to do it. We can pull down a meteor and direct it. Some are so big they will shatter a planet. We don't just create tidal waves."

His look and tone became even more serious, "We are a much smaller force than the Reptoids obviously, but we can knock them out, or any other beings which have turned malevolent for that matter. God's creatures, generally speaking, start out pure as babies do. Then they become corrupt as they develop.

"We, on the other hand, are devoid of any evil. So, if there is a problem in the galaxy, we go in and sort them out. Cosmic cops, that's what we are. We are the governors of space. In fact, we are the kings of space."

"Whom do you answer to?" I asked.

"No one at all, not that I can perceive. We are definitely the lords of space. We have tremendous power and a total sense of right and justice. Perhaps we are God."

"Do you believe in a superior being?" I asked.

"There is a high being, probably God, above all this but I can't define it. I do know exactly why we are here though, we are cosmic cops.

"The dinosaur people have the capability of retaliating. What I can see in my heart is a huge ship that was destroyed by the enemy. You talk about nuclear bombs and missiles on this Earth, they are like pea shooters compared with what goes on up there. This mother ship was blown up almost a million years ago."

I sat up and paid close attention, "Yes, that's it."

"They were here to sort something out and they got clobbered. We brought our fleet of ships here after the mother ship was blown up."

"Did you come to rescue the survivors?"

John waved his arm, "No, they would have stayed anyway, there was no real choice. We came to sort out the Reptoids. In fact, we annihilated them."

Without thinking I blurted out, "Now it's all different. You can't go around blasting people off planets anymore. The hierarchy doesn't want that now. The hierarchy wants peace to prevail throughout the universe by choice, by people experiencing and understanding the energy of love and compassion. Not all of them understand or know it. That's why there are people here who still have an aspect from the dark worlds in them, people who can pick up a gun and kill someone in cold blood and feel no remorse at all."

John frowned, "Galactic beings kicked the Reptoids off the Earth and made man the predominate creature here. But nothing has changed, now man has got completely out of control, he's hopeless."

"When did your ships come here?" I demanded.

"Five years after the mother ship exploded. We came to enforce the edict and they challenged us, so we destroyed them."

Karen screamed in the distance. The sound pulled John from his alpha state. We hurried up the hill to Whale rock. Karen was tossing and turning in the rock cradle. She seemed to be having a vivid recall experience. As we approached, she jumped up from the rock, breathing heavily.

Karen grabbed me, "You lay in that rock and see what I have just seen."

The last thing I wanted to do was to lay in that rock. The events of the day were enough to keep me wondering for weeks. Karen pulled my arm and led me to the cradle.

I sighed and obligingly lay down as she asked. For a moment, I looked up at the blue of the sky, and then closed my eyes. There was a sense of detachment. I was one of many women surrounding her, watching with great interest. Each of us was heavy with child, all volunteers in the great experiment. It seemed Eleura was about to give birth.

It was such an honour to be doing this work. We were bringing light into a world where there was none before. Many of us had been artificially impregnated with our own seed that had been genetically modified to produce a new being, able to cope with the sun and atmosphere of this place. More important, the newborn would be of the light.

The birth came easily, without pain as it always does for **Lyran** women. I looked down to see the child emerge. What came out was covered in dense black matted hair. The newborn struggled to breathe inside its hairy encasement.

The women drew back, screaming with horror, looking at each other with the knowledge that they too might be carrying the same kind of monster within their own bodies. Eleura had to be restrained.

One of the men cut through the matted hair to the little child's face. Its skin was coal black. In our primitive and hurried efforts to produce a viable cross breed with the upstanding ape, we had created something that fell back to a common denominator.

The tiny infant struggled to breathe, its lungs even weaker than our own to the carbon enriched atmosphere.

As I looked at it, I could see that it was of the light in spite of its appearance. The head was also larger, more like our own. The love I felt rushing through me for this child was indescribable.

Several of the women fainted and others ran away crying. I suddenly felt dizzy and unwell, and then sat up. John watched me with a curious expression. Karen stood over me.

"Did you see it?"

"Yes."

"How could we have survived such hardship? All the work we did, only to find ourselves further back than we were before we started. I wanted to kill the child that came from my body. All the women had thoughts they would never have dreamt of before."

Karen wiped tears from her eyes as I pulled myself up, shaking, to my feet. My ears still rang from the sound of the newborn child struggling to breathe. Suddenly I was exhausted, wanting to sleep and cry at the same time. This was enough for one day, "Let's go home, we'll talk about it tomorrow."

That evening John and I attended a charity dinner party. On the patio stood Gerry Bostock, so I walked over to tell him about the events of the day at Kariong. As I opened my mouth to speak, Gerry introduced me to Margaret, an Aboriginal woman. Margaret had read my first book and was quite excited about it.

She took my hand, "You could not have known all that information unless a higher power was working through you. Now that I have met you, I can see that you are over-lighted by a white being. This being is doing its work through you. There is more for you to write about on these matters. Each day will bring you further revelations."

Well, it wasn't over yet, the unusual events of the day were still happening.

Gerry touched my shoulder and winked at me, "You know, we Koori believe that our race is the oldest among humans. We are aware that your anthropologists still theorize the beginnings to be in Africa, but they keep forgetting us, the missing link."

Gerry smiled his warm smile and pointed to the sky above.

"We are star people who have come down through the ages from many parts of the galaxy. As a child, my grandmother would point to the Pleiades and say that was where our ancestors came from. We have no problem believing in the existence of extra-terrestrials, because that is exactly what we are."

The three of us laughed. I looked into their big brown eyes and they were shining with love. This and all the other events of the day seemed to wash over me, until I found myself at home, lying in bed in the quiet of the night, my husband sleeping softly beside me.

This had been quite a day. John had done a scene out of *Star Wars* and expressed every word confidently. I had remembered seeing the birth of a genetic experiment gone terribly wrong, and yet feeling an overwhelming love for that child. Then there was Gerry and Margaret, who had hypnotised me with their Aboriginal charm.

Remembering that tiny black face at Kariong yet again, I was filled with a feeling of love that was quite beyond any I had ever felt.

That woman from long ago was capable of feeling so much more than anything I could imagine. Who was she? Was I really her in that life?

Then as I lay there, I remembered the child dying in anguish four days after its birth, followed by a crushing sorrow, the pushing inside of guilt, the holding in of emotional release. Deep inside, I recognized the same hidden emotions in myself, knowing of them, identifying their cause at last. Could I have carried that for almost a million years? I wanted to cry for that poor infant child, but could not.

John and Valerie Barrow

CHAPTER 4

Alcheringa Talks about
the Children and Birth
Charles Brendon's Regression

Sleep was definitely out of the question. So, it was up to make a cup of hot tea, outside to look up at the stars and find the Pleiades, then back inside to my study to sit with the Alcheringa stone. Better to get the whole story and get on with my life.

Sadly I asked, "Alcheringa, what about the children?" The connection was instantaneous. Alcheringa's voiced was filled with compassion,

"The first batch of new children were not successful, they all died."

"Oh my God", I gasped.

"There was great sadness amongst the mothers, and all who worked to perfect this new race. You must understand, because of the catastrophe of losing the mother ship, the people were stranded in a hostile environment. They suffered horribly with disease, poisons, the extreme heat of the sun, and difficulty in breathing. They did not have the proper equipment to do the job. Because of their situation, they were also not as focused as they could have been or should have been.

"So, they changed their procedures a little, worked faster, and used knowledge gained. The women came forth and volunteered again. Everyone worked very hard with the crystalline light that was imbued into the little unborn children. The new people were called the **Uluru**. It means God's gift. The star people were eventually successful and the Earth is now filled with their progeny."

My eyes burned, "Then why do I feel so guilty?"

"You will have the answer to that soon."

My nose needed a tissue so I thumped around looking for some. Then I remembered my other question, "What about all this Cat people stuff John talked about?"

"Indeed my child, there was a mission with **Siriun** and **Leonine** warriors. They came to Earth to exact retribution for the terrible deed the reptilians had done to the mother ship and the mission. These people had to answer for their actions, and much to the consternation of your little outburst of yesterday, they had to be annihilated. This seems a little harsh, but they had been given a choice. They chose to go back on their word, and for that reason no forgiveness was given. These individuals moved on to other forms, and from there were given assistance."

"And John led this mission?"

"John was then Himel, the Siriun commander. On his ship's arrival at your camp, he reconnoitred the area, just as he re-enacted yesterday at Kariong. He was bitten on the ankle by a snake, another creation of the Reptoids, and was badly affected by the poison. His light was vastly reduced as he went to the edge of death."

*Drawing of the Leonine Star People – **John, or Himel looked more like us as star people although his skull rose higher at the forehead and our skull extended out to the back.***

"The Leonines dispersed themselves around the Earth to eliminate those who acted against the edict of the Elohim. The few surviving reptilians went into hiding in caverns under the Earth.

"Himel was angered, laying helpless in your camp while the Leonines acted. He was unable to understand why he was without power. His weakness confused and upset him a great deal. You and others of the community had learned to overcome these emotions, and were able to assist him.

"Himel became very attached to you my child, and you loved one another. When it came time for the Leonines to move on, he chose to stay with you. There was also the fact that his own light had been so reduced that he would no longer be fully functional in his own society. He knew that he would be more useful by staying on the Earth.

"It was difficult for him, inside he was a warrior, yet the role he played so well was no more."

"When you say loved one another, you mean we had sexual relations?" I asked.

"You did love one another, and became dedicated to each other as well, but you did not have a sexual relationship. The race from which Himel came was an all male race. They reproduced through what you would understand as cloning, it did not take place with a fertilized egg. Their reproduction was a separation from their being into, shall we say, the son of that same being. It was a special process created by mind that was done with permission from the Source. It was a very sacred act. Imagine a piece of energy being pulled away and then replicated. This is what happened within that race of all male energy. It was an advanced way of reproducing."

"Then uh, did they have sex organs?"

"No My Child, they did not. They did have a way of experiencing a frequency in various aspects of their body. This was an uplifting feeling that would tingle through their whole body, similar to a feeling of climax, which immediately connected them to the Source.

"I would like you to understand this because the sexual experience of people on the Earth is actually a way of connecting to the Source, through the love and the fulfilment of that union.

"This is a marvellous gift, a way for the little earthling to come to know and understand God in the deepest and most uplifting way. All they need to understand is where their focus should be. Rather than being on the lower anatomy of the physical body of the human, the focus must be on the heart and love. This is a wonderful way to experience the Source.

"It has a lot to do with intent my child. Sex that is experienced on the Earth will not connect with the Source if it is done with the wrong intent."

I smiled, "Is that why, in spite of the pain, I felt the form of a giant climax, or ecstasy when I gave birth to my children?"

"It is the same."

"What about the marriage between you and me at the time of the mission? How did we have our children? Did we have sex organs?"

"They were there within the physical body that we both wore at that time. We produced children by coming together and uniting in agreement, in desire, and in love of course. The interaction between us was of one of intent. It was a spreading of energy between us, and focusing on what you would call a reproductive organ. They were not quite the same within us, but they were there, and so energy could be focused and held in that part of the physical body."

"When I became pregnant as a star mother with our children, how did the little babies develop?"

"The new being developed in much the same way as an embryo grows within the physical mother of an earthling. It grew within its own little chamber of energy and was nourished by both of us. The consciousness of the unborn child was actually spoken to by both of us, and there was an agreement between the three of us, the mother, the father, and the child. The spirit/soul that was coming into the child was whom we connected and agreed with, to allow that life to come into the embryo. The blueprint for its life and its future were arranged at that time."

"How was the child born? Uh, did I have a vagina?"

"There was not a vagina in the sense of the physical being of the earthling. In many ways, the physical being of the earthling is very similar to the star people, except for this, shall I say, exaggerated development of the sexual organs."

"As a Lyran mother, you grew our first children within your body. There was a line on your body from the navel to the base of the chakra of the spine. At the proper time, this was easily opened, a little like a zipper."

"The child and its amniotic sac was removed, placed into a special receptacle, and allowed to grow until it came time for the sac to break and the child to come forth. This was the result of millions of years of development."

"When the baby was taken from me, it wasn't ready to be born?"

"No my dear, it was nourished and kept under careful observation. It was nourished by light from the Source, and by other Lyran women as well as you. They would nourish the unborn child a little like 'nannies' as it was growing in the amniotic sac. It was kept in a receptacle until a time that was chosen by the little child itself, and then it burst forth. It was a little like coming from an egg."

"In the amniotic sac, it was visible to all. Those that were caring for the little one were very aware and able to communicate and send loving light to it. The little one was born in a more advanced state than the babies that you have in the earthling body. I would say it would be more like a child of four or five years old."

"What happened when we were cast onto the Earth without all this technology available to us?" I asked.

"You did have some technology available to you on the ships that survived. There were many races already understanding this process. The methods that you and the others used on the Earth were not exactly the way that you and I produced our children, but you understood the process.

"An egg was taken from the female volunteers and integrated with cells from the hairy ape like creature, and the two intermingled. There was a force of light that fertilized the egg, and the egg began to split. Because there were difficulties with refrigeration and other technical equipment that was not available, you very quickly implanted the little embryo into the voluntary star mothers. This was done at the base of the stomach through the zip like aspect of that being. It was then held there and nourished until it was time for it to come forth.

"Because of the lack of equipment to continue the growth of the child, the mother continued to carry the little one. It was born prematurely, when still quite small, but it was safe, it still survived.

"With the experimentation that took place, there were adjustments that needed to be made. Cells that were taken from the upstanding ape like creatures could be taken from various parts of their body. Different cells behaved in different ways. This was something that you had to become familiar with, and eventually understood. There was a problem because of the frequency that existed on this Earth. The growth of the newly implanted cell into the little embryo did not perform or change in the same way that you were used to in the worlds from which you came.

"The star people survivors began to understand and adjust to this. There was also information given by the reptilian peoples that came to abide with you. They came because they did not want to be involved anymore with the hierarchy of the Reptoids.

"The first experiments were very difficult and it did not go exactly as planned. However, more experimentation took place, and eventually a new race was created so that a spirit/soul could be absorbed into each new being. Once that was formed, they could then be born into the Earth dimension, and live comfortably within the atmosphere.

"Now you understand this. I am releasing information gradually so that you will understand and see the bigger picture. I am very pleased that you have responded in the way that you have. But then, I agreed to assist you long before you came onto this Earth, and you know this."

I sighed, "Well, it's not quite as horrible as I thought. I think I understand, thank you."

"You are welcome my child, I am very pleased to have imparted this knowledge to you, and I think you are experiencing more with an inner knowing rather than from just the words."

Alcheringa was suddenly gone, and I fell into a light sleep.

The phone rang, and again it was Karen calling.

"Valerie, I've been thinking about it and remembering more. It's different now. I mean we really succeeded after all didn't we? What's important is the outcome. One mistake is just a mistake. With their abilities, I'm certain the star people must have fixed all the others before they were born. I feel better now, how about you?"

"Um, sure," I replied.

"Just think about it, being the ones who gave birth to an entire race. Can you imagine how many descendants we must have?"

Suddenly I felt unwell, "Karen, I can see how you would appreciate that, being a retired elementary school teacher and all. But at the moment, I have a little guilt thing on that subject."

Karen kept right on going, "Well, then you should think about it some more, you need to work this out. I have far greater insight into my life now because of yesterday at Kariong. We should ask Gerry to take us back again, there is so much more to discover."

My head became crystal clear, "Karen, let me work out the arrangements for that. Okay? Christmas will be here in a couple of months, and that would be the perfect time."

"Will you wait on your guilt thing until Christmas?"

"No. I do need to work that out. I'm not sure what to do."

"Why not go see a healer?" suggested Karen.

"A healer for what?"

"Oh, well okay, go see a shrink, just imagine how many different kinds of drugs he will give you to take."

"Alright, I take your point," I relented, "but how can a healer help me?"

"They can help you to release." *Release*, I liked the sound of that word.

An hour went by as we sorted out the possibilities. Gerry had left on a trip to America, so he wasn't available. We settled on Charles Brendon. Karen and I had met him at a seminar. In my memory, he seemed like a nice person, kind of quiet, said he worked in a clinic. I walked around with his phone number for two miserable days before I called him.

"Valerie, I'm so pleased to hear from you. I've been waiting for a long time to work with you."

"You Have?"

"Yes, when we first met I knew we had work to do together." That was kind of convincing, "Charles, I have this problem I ..."

"Why not come and see me, then we can talk about it face to face. Is two o'clock okay for you?"

"Uh, sure, two o'clock sounds fine."

The clinic was more like a cooperative, but was tastefully laid out. The receptionist was efficient, taking me straight to Charles' office.

Charles and I sat facing each other in easy chairs. He seemed to be as I remembered him, a very gentle, almost shy person. For a moment, a feeling of panic descended on me, I had no idea what he was going to do. Well, just lay it out Valerie and see what happens.

"Charles, just recently I had a past-life recall. There is a recollection in particular that is causing me some problems."

"I see," replied Charles, "how did this happen?"

"A new friend took me to Kariong, there are some hieroglyphs cut in the rocks there." I showed a few of the photographs to Charles, "These images seem to evoke memories in people."

Charles nodded as he focused on the photographs.

I continued, "For me, one of the memories was seeing the birth of a child, a kind of experiment that went wrong. The child died after four days, and I have this ..."

A tear ran down Charles' cheek, "Yes, I am aware of a disappointment, yet I can understand why these feelings are there. I feel very strong impressions from these photos, and feelings regarding certain new friends. There is an ancient and familiar bonding."

Charles leaned back in his chair and closed his eyes, "My father stands beside me, waiting for me to loosen the physical body and detach. I am aware of my physical form dying of multiple injuries. There is a pain on my left side.

"Now I am about to be born again into my same mother, how wonderful. This time, I am a newly evolved Earth form. My appearance is contradictory to some, and there are those who are horrified at me. I am born physically hairy, and it hurts to breathe."

Charles sat up and looked straight at me with eyes that seemed filled with extraordinary love and caring, "Wisdom and divine intervention will set the course for the new life forms on Earth. You must forgive yourself, for all creation is God's creation. We must never judge whether one is a mistake or not."

My heart started pounding wildly as Charles continued.

"I did not live very long at that time. You know, in this life until I was four years old, I could not bear for anyone to look at me. Now I understand why."

I desperately wanted tears to run down my face, "I could see the light inside the child. It was of God, and I loved it dearly. I felt the same love for the child I carried."

Charles leaned forward to me, "Yes, and I feel your love as my mother even now. My first Earth experience has reawakened, now I understand."

He had come back. Charles had been my child in that distant time.

Charles took my hands and stood me up, "We are still on a mission to discover and reunite with our family of light and love. It is like a dream come true, only better. Now I feel completion coming with this Earth life. There is excitement and joy, love and peace. These things I am. I give thanks to the Creator's grace and love."

Then Charles took me into his arms and began to sob. I said what I had waited almost a million years to say, "I'm so sorry." He cried and cried, at times like a child. I wanted to as well, but could not. Yet, inside I felt good, the heartache was gone.

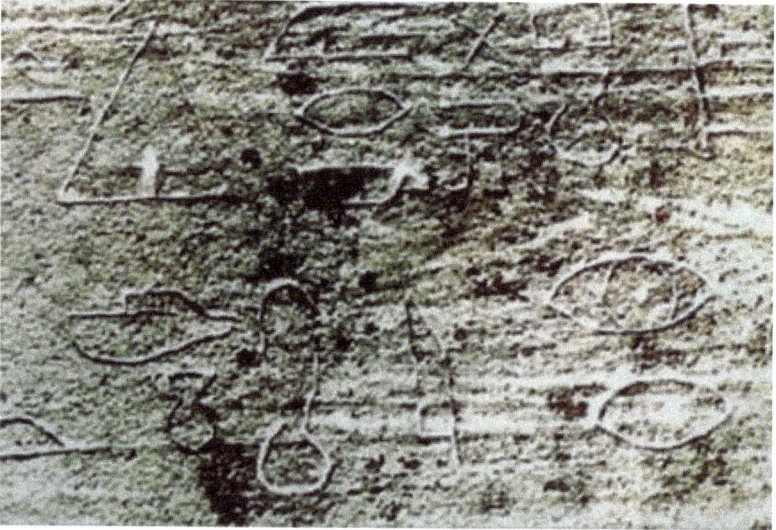

CHAPTER 5

Candice's Regression
James and Tricia's Regression
Rosalyn's Regression
Egarina introduces herself

Charles' departing words echoed in my mind, "Gather the star family, help them rediscover their celestial heritage and fulfil their part in the Almighty's unfolding dream."

Is this my mission, the work I am supposed to do in this life? Charles seemed to think so.

Did he heal me or did I heal him? I'm not exactly sure what happened in that office, but I felt much better. At the same time, I suspected there was an agenda at work.

On the trip home, I stopped at the market. As always, I checked out with my favourite grocery checker.

"How are things at Alcheringa, Valerie?" asked Susan. "Moving right along," I answered, still reflecting on the events of the day.

While stuffing the bags into the trunk of my car, a young woman came up to me. "Excuse me, my name is Candice, I was standing in line behind you."

"Yes I remember."

"Well, ah, the word Alcheringa means something to me."

I smiled, "It does?"

"Yes, well, I have this sort of dream. Oh, you'll probably think this is crazy."

"Not at all, tell me," I replied, oblivious. She looked around nervously. I suggested that we sit in my car, which we did.

Candice took a deep breath, "I have this recurring dream where I see a black man standing on one leg, you know in the Aboriginal fashion. He balances himself with a long spear and then asks me to remember who I was. He says his name is Alcheringa, and then he gives me a message."

"Yes," I replied.

The strangest look came over her face, "The message is that my soul has some information for you."

Well, I was stunned. After what had happened earlier with Charles, I thought nothing could faze me. Now a complete stranger was doing it again. I took the pictures from my handbag, "Look at these Candice, see if there is anything that attracts you or seems familiar."

Candice didn't need the pictures. Her eyes began to close.

"Yes, I remember now. There is a large silvery ship. It is very bright inside. There is a big room filled with many people. We are just waiting for the commander. There he is now, we all cheer and clap. It's amazing because none of the people are moving their hands or mouths. We seem to be able to make these sounds with just our minds. We are all in telepathic communication. Everyone is so happy, the mission is just wonderful."

"What does the commander say?" I asked.

"He says we are going to a new world to bring light and love where there is none. We are all here by our own choice. If you feel hesitation, you are free to leave now before we depart for the new world. We go to a place with one sun, many light years away, and life will no longer be as you have known it. If everyone is ready to go, we will leave now."

Candice paused, seeming to wait for my question.

"Tell me what is happening," I said.

"The doors are all closing as the commander leaves for the bridge. The people sit in repose. Sitting in a sleep state helps them to adjust to the new atmosphere."

"Are there children around?"

"Of course, I am one of them. We are somewhere else."

"Are you a boy or a girl?" I asked.

Candice ducked her head under her blouse, looking from side to side with closed eyes, "It feels soft, so I must be a girl."

"What is your name, are you with your family?"

"*Chay-ra-ring.* I have no family on board. I am old enough to leave on my own. My role is to travel and find new worlds. I am excited about that. I have a good mind for communication. Now I feel as if I am in a trance, I seem to be in a cylinder."

Her body shuddered, "The ship is broken, and things don't work."

I did not want to have her crying in my car at a supermarket, "Move on in your memory, see yourself walking on the new planet."

Candice sighed and relaxed, "I see a dark face. I am beautiful and I have hair too. My body is dark with skin like silk. There is hair on my arms, but very fine. My hands have thick fingers."

"Who are you with?"

"There are others around, looking after each one."

"What do the people do for food?"

"We eat fruit from trees, nuts, and grass seeds. We live in caves warm from the Earth. Mother keeps us warm. Our mother is the Earth. We gather food and all work as one. Men and women work the same, there is no difference."

"We dance in ceremony, thanking the big yellow sun and mother Earth for all that is provided."

"Do you know where your forefathers came from?" I asked.

"Yes, from the stars. All the stars have names, they teach us. The hunting ground, our food, everything is by the stars."

"Can you remember how long ago your forefathers from the stars came here?"

Candice gestured with her arms, as if talking to someone.

"Grandmother cannot remember them being here, but she says her mother knew them. Their skin could not take the sun. Time passed, and they all died."

I asked her how the babies were born, and she began slapping her stomach. Then I asked, "How did the baby get there?"

She pointed with her other hand, "From him over there, the big one, he looks after me." Candice then seemed to drift into a sleep state.

This young woman had walked into my life to give me the second lesson of the day. Yeah, there was definitely an agenda at work.

After a few minutes, Candice opened her eyes, seeming a little disappointed, "What just happened here?"

I told her about the others and myself. Candice let out a little sigh, realising that she was not the only one. After giving her my card, I invited her to attend one of my meetings.

For some time, I had been holding a work group at my house once a month. The idea is to allow others to ask Alcheringa questions.

When I returned home, James and Tricia were waiting for me. They are both actors, very New Age kind of kids. They had come to ask Alcheringa some personal questions. This time I was awake, so my ears were pricked up.

John was on the phone, energetically cutting a business deal, so we walked into the bush, pausing at a place we all agreed would be right for the channelling. I placed the Alcheringa stone on the ground and we settled ourselves around it. I saw myself, in my mind's eye, sitting on top of Uluru, calling Alcheringa's name softly. He came with quite a loud and earthy energy, along with a sense of fun.

Alcheringa pre-empted most of James' and Tricia's questions, requesting that they look within for more understanding of the things that were troubling them. When he left, I felt there was still more work to do, there was that pushing feeling inside of me again.

James seemed disappointed and got up, telling us he was returning to the house. Tricia and I just sat together for a while. Then I felt Alcheringa enter into me again to speak, "Tricia, feel the energy of the ship Rexegena. See yourself as a little girl, sitting on a box of crystalline energy. The box is a silvery colour and it feels warm. You are very young."

Tricia smiled. Her eyes looked away into the distance for a moment, and then closed.

"I feel very comfortable sitting here, looking out through the viewing port into space. It's a very familiar place. There are many people around wearing blue suits. They have long heads, and they're working at this board, a computer control kind of thing. I'm there as a guest, just having fun. There is no one looking after me, it's like I have come of my own accord and I am welcomed.

"My father is the commander-in-chief of the Rexegena. My mother, that's you Valerie, is the communicator, wearing a crystal on her head that amplifies the telepathic communications to our home base in the Pleiades.

"As I look out the window, I can see energy patterns projected out in front of the ship. We are moving towards this energy pattern. It is a gateway. The gateway has two spiralling forms, and we are waiting for the right time to move into them. There is a great sense of expectation. Everyone is very excited about travelling into the gateway. It is not the right time yet, because there is an alignment that needs to take place within the energy pattern. It also has to do with the consciousness of the ship.

"I am moving off the silver box now, and down towards a special capsule. I step into this capsule, which helps elevate the energy levels as we travel into another dimension on the ship.

"I feel myself moving out of my body as it lies in the capsule. Now I see myself out of my body, and moving into an area where there are other souls. It is a meeting.

"When my body is in the capsule, there is a liquid crystal around it. This crystal keeps the body on one level of consciousness, frozen in time. It allows you to sleep while you travel around.

"I am in my light form, a subtle white and gold ovoid that has many coloured rays going through it, like meridians. I am still a young girl, in that this is my function, but my consciousness is more expansive. I have chosen to take on this identity in order to hold energy for the purpose of the ceremony we are going into.

"Other people are there, many families as light beings, for they have left their bodies too. Our focus extends toward the meridian lines, and we all connect with each other to form a circuit. We use this to program the ship to enter the gateway. We don't move into the gateway, we are suddenly just through it. There is no linear movement as such, we are just instantly there.

"I am back in my body now. The skin is a bluish white colour and luminous. My hands are long and slender with three fingers and a thumb." Tricia grinned broadly, "I have very big eyes and a long head. I have no teeth, it seems like just gums.

"I feel someone from my family calling out, it's my brother looking for me. When I find him, he is very frightened, sensing that something is not right. He is very connected to energies. I feel worried for him, as I know he has the ability to see things in the future. I tell him to be quiet and not to tell anyone. It's okay to have secrets between us that we don't tell. Yet, I feel guilty for not letting him express it.

"There are fields around the vessel that we have to maintain. I want to leave that energy field, I feel trapped in there. My brother feels trapped as well. We know how to get out, but we have to stay because of our family. We have to go with them.

"We are getting close to our destination now, and I sense the danger my brother feels. After we arrive, the feeling becomes very intense and I fear for my brother's life.

"I choose to act in defiance, placing my brother into an escape capsule, and then ejecting him towards the planet.

Then I enter my sleeping capsule to travel and find out what is wrong. I am jolted by the pain and anguish of thousands of my people from the shock of a massive explosion. Now I feel separated from them.

"Why are you separated?" I asked.

"Because I'm out of my body. My body is back in the capsule, and it's still sleeping. I can't get back in there. The Rexegena is destroyed.

"I am moving away from that as everything is all gone. My body in the capsule was not destroyed because it was in that liquid. I can't get back in, and now I feel guilty. I feel as if I should have been in there. My body is being used, those people have my body.

"What happens?" I asked.

"I come back to Earth in another body, and I can see that my old body is still there, being used by the Reptoids. They are trying to get the light particles from my body, but they can't work out the coding."

She laughed as if it were extremely amusing, "They want to reproduce the body. They want to use the cells to create other creatures. They want to use it against my family, against the star people. I laugh because they can't do it, and now I am back to claim my body.

"The body I am in now is big and strong, and my head is really flat. It's feline and cat like. I come with the Alcheringa stone, and I am tempted to give it to these Reptoids in exchange for my little child body. I tell them they can encode their work and their history into the stone, and that it can be used to unite people. But I don't give it to them; I give it to a child to take care of."

"What child, a Reptoid child?"

"No, it's my brother. He's in a new body that has been engineered here on Earth. This is a lot later. He is humanoid, but very white and he stays under the ground. He is so cute, and he remembers me too.

"We think it's very funny because I am now in this big strong body, and he is in a little body. I give the stone to him. He has to intone the stone for some sort of communication.

"His head is big and he is white with blue eyes. He has a bit of very fine hair and he's tiny. There are calcium deposits in him that I am not used to. His skin is very flaky. My family created him, the star people family.

"My mother is still there, but she is not my mother now because I am in a different body. My brother is no longer my brother because he is in a different body as well."

"Where are the star people?"

"A lot of them have died. There is a small group left, but they won't live much longer. They have agreed to work with a few of the Reptoids that came to them."

"Who created these new beings?"

"Well originally the star people created them, but there has been engineering going on by the Reptoids. The Reptoids under the Earth have been able to reproduce the crystalline substance that was around my body, but they haven't been able to reproduce the body itself, and then manipulate that body."

"Describe the Reptoids."

"I am watching this one and he's very scaly and dry with some hair. His face protrudes out, so that he looks like a lizard. They have lumpy things on the side of their heads where ears should be, and they have humped backs. The Reptoids have web like hands with three fingers and claws. I am talking to one of them. I am actually trying to get my body back from him. I even threaten him, for I have a team with me, an army who look just like I do."

"What do you look like?"

"I look like a lion kind of person. All of us have hairy manes, and furry red arms. We have big eyes with yellow gold inside. They appear to be black, but you can see a glow inside of them. Our coats are coloured more like a tortoise shell colour. My hands have a skin covering, but there are pads on the underneath and pads on the knuckles as well. There is a retractable claw on the fourth finger and another claw further down nearer the palm. We use the claws for fighting.

"There are fifteen other warriors with me, and I am their leader. I am male. We travelled from the Pleiades, although we are not originally from there. Others are on board our ship as well as the lion people. They are big too, with long heads and large eyes. They drive the ship and wear blue navy uniforms."

This was familiar ground, "Who is the Commander of the ship?"

She began to laugh, "Its John!"

This would be a major correspondence, "The same John that is my husband now?"

Tricia chuckled and smiled, "Yes, but here his name is Himel. I don't like him very much because I think he is arrogant. I have a reasoning process, and he has this 'Let's go kill people and blow things up' attitude. He really doesn't want to reason, he just wants revenge. I want to reason things out. I want to play a tactical game."

"The Lion people that are on the ship, are you related to one another?" I asked.

"We are, but it is not considered important really, it is more a knowing that we are all connected. We don't have a family structure."

"So, if there were new babies created, how does that happen?"

"It happens through physical intercourse. It is very strange because that is the first time I have ever experienced anything like that. It was a very new experience. There is always love, caring, humour, and a beautiful warmth amongst us. The lion people are travellers and very masterful warriors. We are able to consciously connect with each other through a language that is more of a signal, a kind of movement, very subtle with our eyes and our bodies. There is a lot of posturing that indicate things to each other; in warfare particularly, and in our negotiation processes."

"Who do you answer to when a war has to take place?"

"The higher council of light, we act in their service. The Lion people came at this time to assist those star people who had been trapped on Earth. We were also instructed by the higher council to remove the Reptoids. We are prepared to fight them if they don't leave, but set out in tactical ways, as I want to reason with them. We all want to get them off the Earth. We actually do have a big war, destroying many thousands of them. It was near where Africa is now."

"Did any of your race lose their lives?"

"Yes, but that was what we went there for."

"Are any of those off the starship, like Himel, involved in the war?"

"No, they came to make a presentation, to make an offer of truce, but they don't even get off the ship. We, the Cat people, go first, and then war breaks out."

"Are you aware if pieces of the mother ship came to the Earth?"

"It sort of melted. There were pieces all around. It was organic. I could see some of it under the water in the south, but I couldn't say exactly where. This place is beautiful, it's so green, and the water is so blue."

"How do you leave the Earth?"

"I travel with my little brother to try and find his creators, the star people. We are looking for the bay again."

"Do you find it?"

"He does, but I die along the way."

"There is a song about the ignorance of the little earth-lings. It's a beautiful sound that creates a wonderful vibration throughout the universe. It is like a rainbow.

"The five, and the seven, and the twelve people who have incarnated on Earth represent different aspects of the rainbow. Their ignorance is like a conductor that will tell them how to play themselves, so that they will change and swap between their seven-chakra systems. When they do this, it will create a magnetic pole within their central being. This will attract some people towards them, and repel other people away as it creates a new rhythm. I might be purple at one time, someone else will be blue, and we come together to create this new rhythm. This will create yet another colour, which will open a gateway into a new realm.

"The quickening is about our conductors, our ignorance, coming together to form the one identity. This presents revelations to us. Our ignorance is actually controlled by our intuition and our higher self; when these come together, new information is given, creating an ascension."

Tricia opened her eyes, "Hmm, that was interesting, I could see all the colours as they interacted."

Her description of the song puzzled me, "What does the song thing you talked about mean."

Tricia smiled an almost Mona Lisa smile, "It doesn't matter, the information is for the light being within you, it has been told again to remind you. Now you should talk to James."

We returned to the house.

Photo of rocks near Kariong hieroglyphs. Note rocks resembling the Dolphin and the Lion, representing our 'rescuers'

James settled into a chair to get on with the work. He quickly moved into the memory of being a little boy on the ship Rexegena.

From the beginning of the journey, he felt anxious, sensing danger with a strong sense of trouble ahead. He didn't want to tell anybody about it, but confided in his sister, knowing she could feel it too.

"You don't feel you can tell anyone?" I asked.

"No, I kind of know that it isn't for me to tell. I am not given any information from the source. I just know something is going to happen in a different time zone. I'm not able to see the physical manifestation of that feeling. This is a new thing for me, and it wouldn't help to have that visual inside of my head.

"I still feel some discord, which I would relate to here on Earth in the now as anxiety. It is a new sensation for the body I am in. While I am reasonably comfortable with this anxiety, it is a heavy weight to carry around. Now it now limits my ability to access certain frequencies within my heart, I have this limitation."

It seemed as if he were talking as an Earth being in the now of what his heart is made up of. I asked him to go onto the ship and further into the memory of the little boy and what he looked like.

"I am quite small. My hands are long with three fingers and a thumb. My skin is blue with an opalescent sheen."

"Is your mother's skin the same?"

"No, hers is almost white like light, it glows. My father's is white as well. Father has a gold disk that hovers around his head, and spheres that run up his spine on the outside. Mother has a crystalline rod that is connected to the disk around her head. That's what they look like to me."

"Do you see them differently than others see them?"

"Uh, yeah I guess so. I can see them in many forms, but this is the form that they in are at the moment."

"You seem to have a strong connection to your sister."
"Yeah."

"Why is that?"

He laughs, "That's a big question, it would take me ages to answer."

"What is your earliest memory of being a little boy?"

"My body being created from a subtle gas of sub-atomic particles in a cylinder. The configuration of my real self is as a spirit of light. I am seeing now how my physical body is being created. Around me are other beings, including myself, but I am not yet in a physical form. While the new form is taking place in the gases within the cylinder, it can't be seen yet in physical reality. We are creating this physical body. In terms of its function, it is only a vehicle. Even I am helping to create this system, as my new body is an experimental prototype.

"I see myself coming into that body. Because it does not yet exist in a physical form, my light body takes over and it goes like a line printer zip-zip-zip. The legs start appearing, then zip-zip-zip upwards, and the head appears. It's as if I kick-start a hologram, for that's all it really is. Finally, there I am, a little boy."

"What part do your mother and father play in this creation?"

"You and he pass on knowledge. Both of you have great knowledge in the forms that you are in. There is a ceremony. It's quite complicated to talk about right now. I don't have the exact terms."

"Are cells or atoms used from your parents?"

"In part, but it's not so much on the physical level where there is a connection with them. There is another level before that, a vibration of light frequency that is more a choosing to manifest.

"I am primarily **Arcturian**, seeded by a mother and father who are not Arcturian. This is entirely possible. It is something that we can do."

This was very confusing, "Your mother and father are not Arcturian?"

"No."

"Do you know were they came from? Do your mother and father come from the same place?"

James thought about it for a long time, looking a little confused, "Uh, no they don't, but there is something very similar about them. It seems I can't remember."

"You seem a little lost. That's okay, you're only a little boy, and you feel a sense of imminent danger. Are you able to bypass that and enjoy the trip?"

"Oh yes of course, I am with many amazing beings, I am having so much fun. There are people from all over the place. I talk and communicate. I have a beautiful connection with everyone on board. I am allowed to walk around everywhere, with access to all levels of consciousness on the ship."

"Is there a place to eat on the ship?"

"There is a place we go to during regular intervals, an energy point. I see a big glowing cylinder with a light that shoots off it. Everyone there is standing around it, and it feels as if we are sitting down to dinner.

"Other than that, I just move around the ship communicating with people and having little ceremonies with everybody. I'm really enjoying myself."

"Can you describe the ship?"

"Words can't really tell you exactly what it is. Mathematical equations would explain it better. I can somewhat describe the dimension of it. It isn't like a solid vessel, as if it were only in three dimensions. It is always in motion, it is a living entity, and there is a consciousness within it. Human beings find it hard to perceive that a form can exist at other levels of consciousness. The mother ship is massive. The physical form is a kind of sphere, but it has bits that came off and change it all the time.

"The Rexegena isn't like a space ship that just travels in a linear way, it is multi-dimensional and it can move through zero points. The ship can travel through time and space instantly. It is a remarkable piece of technology, state of the art stuff."

"What do you do when you need to have a rest?"

"I just stop and go into myself."

"Do you need to go into a capsule?" I asked.

His tone became serious, "I have to go into the capsule because it is connected to a generator. I am also placed into the capsule when we need to make a move. While my body is asleep, the physical part acts as a vessel for a frequency of light to come through. This is conducted through my consciousness, and flows through this connection to a generator that projects the ship into another place. I am not doing this alone, there are quite a few of the young ones who do this."

"You are doing this even though you are only a little boy?"

His answer startled me, "Being a child has nothing to do with it, we propel the ship."

For a moment, I reflected on his last statement, star children propelling a giant mother ship through a gateway. Then I asked him to move further into the memory of the little boy who feared for the future. He appeared to be feeling almost unwell, knowing that he was carrying the knowledge of a dangerous event in his heart, one that was getting closer.

"I only told my sister, she asked me to keep it secret, and well, she is like my guardian."

"What happens at the event that is upsetting you?"

"I have been ejected out from the mother ship. I was placed in an escape capsule and my sister ejected me. As I am projected downwards towards the planet, I see stuff flying everywhere. I am watching this from both psychic and physical reality points. I can see an electromagnetic force beam shooting into the ship and eventually blowing it up.

"I am scared and sad, yet relieved. The event has finally happened, although it is horrible. I am witnessing destruction like I have never imagined before. Then I feel the presence of my sister inside of me, reassuring me that everything is perfect. She tells me there is nothing to fear, and that I will be greeted on my arrival. I feel her love so strongly that I am no longer afraid.

"I am being drawn into the atmosphere. It is daytime when I land in trees at the edge of a sea. I get hurt but am able, while still in my capsule, to heal myself. When I emerge, playful dolphins expecting my arrival greet me. I am having trouble breathing, so they take me into the sea, teaching me how to breathe and swim under the water. They teach me to shift my shape into a dolphin body. It feels wonderful. I didn't know this was going to happen.

"I can still feel the pain of all the people that do survive. I sense they are having a bad time. This is hard for me as an Arcturian. It is so foreign trying to cope with the pain and trauma of the others. But at the same time, I am having a lot of fun with the dolphins because they are such loving creatures. We exchange a lot of information about the Earth. We embed knowledge into the crystals that are buried deep under the ocean. These crystals are still there, stuff to do with the zodiac, the cycles of the moon, the sun, and the planets.

"I stay for four seasons, setting the electromagnetic-consciousness grids of the Earth, the webs. I can see the geometric net around the Earth. I am also communicating with my sister in an archetypal form, for we are brother and sister, we are the same. She is travelling all over the place to different planets."

"What happens after the four seasons with the dolphins?"

"I become a bird for a brief period of time, because I still have the knowledge of shape-shifting. I can see a massive bird that has a kind of prehistoric tinge to it. It has a great consciousness. I am in that body for twelve months. I fly around the colony that has been established by the star people, the ones that survived. They know I am there, and I am regarded as a good omen. I am in communication with my mother and it is beautiful.

"She has started to recover. The star people are mastering new forms, understanding them so that they can have a law. They are trying to write the book so to speak. This is a metaphor for understanding the essential principles of reality in terms of creating, in terms of matter manipulation. There are new ethics, new laws in this dimension. They are mapping these, actually putting them to the test, and just exploring. They are doing very well at it, and learning quite quickly.

"A lot of time passes. Many new forms have been created by the settlement. There is quite a bit of progression."

"They aren't just creating hairy ones?" I asked.

"No, this is after that. After the first hairy ones were created, there were more creations. It was kind of like you created one race, then more, and now there are five races. There is a lot of mixing, matching, and formulating going on, like let's try this and then that."

As he spoke, I could sense the mixing and matching, with different sizes, colours, and levels of spirituality. What an incredible undertaking this must have been. An understanding came to me of the variable nature of humankind.

"Now I am in a little white man's form, I am quite motionless. I don't feel much. There are many worlds under the Earth, and there is even a source of light. It is magical but it is all deserted. There are altars, palaces, and rivers. I am down there for a while, tuning music into the crystals under the Earth, using the twelve patterns from the planets surrounding the Earth. I am like a conductor, although there are many ethereal beings working with me.

"I eventually leave the Earth on a ship that the Cat people take back to Sirius A. Now I am in the corps, the corps of the sun, with the same white body. I am able to survive there."

"What can you tell me about that?"

"Well I can talk about just anything. I've been all around the galaxy."

"Tell me more about being that little boy on the star ship just before the explosion. How did you know this was going to happen?"

James's face grew dark and he came out of his alpha state. He wanted to hold back information that was inside him, avoiding facing the pain of that little boy on the ship. When I voiced that, he became upset as if I didn't understand him, and then jumped up from the chair saying he had to go. He took Tricia's hand and almost ran to his car.

Gee, this one was different, he ran away.

Rosalyn was the next one who came to view the pictures of Kariong and sit in the "hot seat." When she responded to them, I asked her to see herself in the mothership leaving the Pleiades.

"I am looking at a corner space in this room, even though the ceiling curves down to the walls. All of the fittings seemed to be moulded. It's a bit like a cabin on a ship, only different. There is a light on my left hand side that is controlled by my mind. If I think of lying down, an invisible energy table appears, and I lie on it. I seem to be able to lie down horizontally with nothing underneath me. It feels quite hard to me, yet my mind is holding it there.

"When I want to lie down I go up to it, think I am weary, and it appears as if to welcome me. It tucks away when I have finished sleeping.

"I have a short skirt on. My legs are very thin and long. I am wearing stockings that are a mauve grey colour. I seem to have boots up to the calf, but when I get onto the energy table, I don't have my boots on anymore. I didn't see myself taking them off. The energy table is about waist high, somewhat higher than a normal bed. I am not getting into it like a bed, I'm just lying on top.

"We use a mental process to rest. It's all done with thought. I wave my hand in front of the light and the energy field forms as I think about it. I go into a mental process as I lie on the energy field. I focus on rest and nothing else. I control the flow of blood and the flow of nutrients to my organs. The mind consciously puts my body to sleep. I might do this for two hours. If I have no interaction for eight hours, I will stay in a state of suspended animation for that length of time.

"This is so different to when I go to bed in this life. People seem to have forgotten how to do this. Now I think of a million things before I go to sleep. We just trust that if we close our eyes, we will go to sleep. The chemicals in our brain are now what put us to sleep, it has become instinctive. We don't consciously blink our eyes anymore. They just blink by themselves. Everything is now an instinctive process.

"As I lie there I am very aware of the process of sleep. I am in control, so it is not an instinctive process. We put ourselves into a state of suspended animation, and also establish how long we want to be asleep. This can vary according to our next duty roster, or our next interaction. An interaction can be a service function or a social function such as a meeting with a friend. It can also be to perform something for the colony.

"We regard ourselves as a colony on this ship. We don't think of ourselves as separate. In any interaction that is to take place, everyone else knows about it. Every interaction is for the benefit of all, and makes everybody happy. Nothing is performed that would be out of harmony with the rest of the colony. We have a hierarchy in the colony that is just like ants. There are workers, thinkers, teachers, and those that look after the children. This is because their parents don't. Well, I mean they do, but they don't. Nobody owns the children. Even the parents aren't responsible for the children, the colony is.

"This consciousness is very different, a little bit like the indigenous races on Earth, where the children of the tribe have all the females as aunts, or the males as uncles. Everybody corrects the children and looks after them. The parents that give birth to the children are not necessarily their educators."

"Do you have family on-board or a husband?"

"I am fairly young, and I have a sense that there is a child. Yet, I am alone in this room."

"After you sleep for a while, what happens?"

"Now it is time to get up. As I do, I feel this energy shield slide back from around me. It's as if I have been in a cocoon. When I get up, I wave my hand across the light, and the cocoon slides away. You can program the cocoon as you want, and you can be in there for a hundred years if you like. There is a fluid atmosphere inside that provides nourishment while you rest.

"Now I am up and I have my boots back on. I am wearing a top that is very shiny, silvery, with epaulettes that come out from the top of the shoulders. My arms are covered in the same colour and material as my legs. I have very small breasts."

"What do you do when you have to go to the toilet?"

"It seems I don't ever do that. I pull my skirt up and look down to see my genitals. My body seems to be hairless. There is something that could be called a vagina I guess. It's just a line down there. There is a cord, like an umbilical cord hanging down. But it's not coming from the navel, it's coming from inside of me.

"Maybe it's an extension of the urethra, or even a clitoris. It's seems to be like plaited or twisted flesh. I don't think the cord is for excreting because we live on different stuff here. That's all there is, just this cord.

"But how would you reproduce?"

My last reading with Alcheringa came to mind, "Can I suggest that the line that you think is a small vagina is something that can be opened up just like a pocket?"

"Well I am wondering if the baby just pops out."

"That is exactly what I am suggesting," I said. "Look at the line that goes down from the navel to where the vagina would be. Can this be opened up with the mind so that a baby can be implanted, and then closed up again to live from the nutrients that you give it? When the time is right, can you literally unzip the tummy, take the baby out, and put it in one of those cocoons to grow further?"

"I don't know. This is very confusing because there doesn't seem to be a vagina that a man would put his penis in. There is an exchange of energy between the male and female. It's very important, the finger tips.

"Wait, I just had a memory. If you want to be extremely intimate with someone, you just put both hands up and join all the fingertips to the partner's fingertips. Now all your meridians are interlocked, and there is like a flowing of your juices. You wouldn't do that with just anybody, this is intimate. This is done only with someone you are really close to. You can do it with three fingers with someone else. One hand crossed in front of your chest to meet the opposite upright hand of another is considered a warm welcome. This is 'hello', or 'how are you?' But all the fingertips connecting with the fingertips of another is only for lovers."

What a lovely insight this was. Rosalyn seemed to be in rapture at the memory of it.

"This greeting is for the dearest one. All of your feelings are in your hands. It's so open hearted. There is nothing to hide, and you are in complete agreement.

"I am trying to remember giving birth to a child as a star person. I can easily remember the intimacy that I felt with my lover when we touched hands. But I can't connect in the same way with a memory of giving birth. I know that my breasts are important. The breasts produce a kind of nectar. In my breasts, there is a particular gland on the inside of the breast here."

Rosalyn pointed to an area of her breast just to the inside and above the nipple, "It's like they produce this nectar. I feel that in a good mother there is a natural process where the milk is enriched with this nectar of the Gods.

"The most important nourishment the child needs is love. We are more concerned with the child receiving love than physical nourishment. In our society today, we have become more concerned with the physical nourishment than the spiritual. For those of us on the mother ship, love is the most important. We know that forms of higher evolution must produce love if our species is to continue evolving.

"I feel pleased because my glands are working well. I brought my child with me onto the mother ship. I remember that whenever I am feeding, I am giving the right nourishment. We have to have our nectar analysed to make sure it has the right amount of gold energy. If the baby doesn't get this, it will mutate. The nectar seems to be fed to the embryo down a sort of tube inside my body that connects to the inner sac inside the tummy. I can't feel anything on the inside of my tummy because it is so different from a human placenta inside a body. It was inside a pouch that could be opened up. It's a bit like the way birth operates for female marsupials. I can feel my breasts and the nourishment coming from my heart.

"What was important for the sisters in the clinic was to check on the energy that was being fed to the child, so that its potential was allowed to develop. It was like they were frightened that if the child were not fed the love energy, they would mutate back into a war-like race. We wanted our species to evolve and always live in love."

"Who is the war-like race that they were concerned about? I asked.

"Oh. Well, it's Orion. They were always fighting us."

"Why would the babies mutate back if Orion wasn't of your race?"

"I don't know."

"Move on in your memory. You have come out of your cabin and are heading towards an interaction," I suggested.

"There are some people that I have to meet. Many plants are growing in a hothouse. I am meeting with two people to talk about these plants. One person is definitely male and he is much bigger than we are. The other is female but she is a bit blurred. They are dressed differently than me. They wear brown according to their function. It has something to do with these plants. Ah, they are botanists.

"The man has a very full forehead and heavy bone structure across the eyes. His eyes are inset in a nice open face that is wide across the forehead. He has a fairly big mouth with full lips, and nostrils that flare a little bit. There is no hair. He has lovely broad strong hands, and his skin is a creamy caramel colour.

"They are telling me about trying to prepare crops that will grow in the colony when we get to Earth. They are trying to create certain life forms that will produce these crops. This is the food that we will be able to eat, because we've been told that we can't eat the food on Earth. It's too dense. The hierarchy told us that."

I asked her to find the ship's commander and describe him.

"I am seeing the Commander in two different forms. First, I see him in boots and close fitting suit type dress. Next, I see him in a robe with a chain. This is probably what he wears to ceremonies.

"We have assemblies, and he comes and gives regular talks to prepare us for where we are going. There is a lot of adaptation to our bodies that need to take place. There are many things to understand about what we have to face. We have been told that there are other life forms on the planet we are going to. We are told the vegetation is different. Our vegetation is teal blue. On the Earth, it is green.

"We are told that there is a lot of water, and there are life forms that live in the water, such as dolphins. We can communicate with them, and they will help us. We know this because there has been interaction with them before. This happened on our star ships from Sirius.

"We have come to colonise and bring love. This energy is not on the planet, and we have agreed to do this to help the life forms to evolve. We all feel good about this. It is part of our service for the Creator. The only way to know the Creator is through love and service. We love all, and serve all.

"There is one little memory that is very clear and I would like to say it. It was after we had been on Earth for a while, and had been through great hardships. There was one Reptoid who was helping us. I was amazed at how well this Reptoid was adapted to the Earth situation. He was able to cope with the environment better because his skin was different than ours. He was able to do so much more than we were, because we were so delicate. I wished that I were more like him. There was so many times that this same thought came up. It seemed to be so repetitious.

"This is because he could cope with emergencies, and he didn't have any dramas in his life. He just lived and tackled whatever he was doing. Nothing to him was an emergency or a drama. Nothing valued was more important than anything else. Everything was just an action to God. He made my life easier to live because he had the ability to cope with being on Earth so much better than I could.

"He was of great assistance, and he did things that kept us alive. This was simple for him, but very difficult for us. His skin was very tough and scaly like a crocodile. It was suitable for the Earth's conditions, much more so than our skin, which tore easily and was very fragile.

"In this life, I've always thought that reptilian skin was repulsive, yet in my memory I rather admired it for its usefulness in the Earth's climate. I remember an incredible gratitude to him for his protection, and I know he loved me very much. He thought my form was exquisite, and he loved my skin. He saw his work for us as service to God.

"What is also very important for me to remember is the botany. As part of my service I was responsible for tending the plants, and bringing them to the Earth so that we would have food to eat."

Rosalyn sat up and looked at me with amazement, "That's why I want to feed everybody in this life. I don't think I ever quite got over that. If there is a food shortage because of Earth changes, I'll understand why I feel so strongly that I have to do it."

As Rosalyn was leaving my house, a new kind of aura came over me. I went to my study and sat with the Alcheringa stone. The voice that spoke through me this time was soft and female.

"I am *Egarina*. I have come this day to present myself to you. Do not be afraid. Many from the star worlds are here.

"See the ocean, the way it moves in and out. There is movement in everything. Even the mother Earth moves. Her breath comes in and out just as the tides. There is a constant movement of energy. Take this energy into you, breath it in and out. There is a wonderful flowing gentleness, and if all is well within you, nothing to obstruct that energy flow. You come and you go much the same as the breath. Do you understand?"

Her voice was soothing and I relaxed, "Yes, I think so."

"There is another aspect of you, as there is with everybody. From that point, you operate with more knowledge and understanding. The body is transitional, it has a very limited life. A personality however, is a line that is descendant. It really does not matter what dimension it operates in. The knowingness and the knowledge will still operate, whether it is through the personality that you are now or another. You come from that point of knowingness, so there is no limit." Egarina laughed softly. "But not to rush out because you hear of other things my dear, stay where you feel right within your heart."

Even her humour entranced me, this woman with a manner that was so gentle.

"I am here to remind people of who they are and how they are connected with the cosmic races. While the body they walk in is the race of the earthling, it is not all that they are."

"Why do you do this?" I asked.

"This is the completion of an agreement I made nearly one million years ago, a promise that one day I would come back when the time was right. This was given while leaving my body at that time. I had begun to see and understand what the bigger plan was all about, in creating a race with warmth, love, and peace in their hearts. It is they who will help to change the energies upon this Earth.

CHAPTER 6

Stephen's Regression
Michael's Regression
Joseph's Regression

I need to trust and let things take their own course, as long as it feels right. Don't try to control it Valerie, ask for guidance, and wait for the star people to come to you.

So, along comes Steven.

Steven is a talented oil painter in his early twenties. He is very tall, quite sensitive, and a medium. I met him when he came to one of my meetings. When I showed him photos of the hieroglyphs, he was captivated.

He recalled a dream where, as the painter Raphael, he remembered cutting some of the hieroglyphs into the chasm walls in another time.

He felt he was in the chasm and could sense Raphael's presence, as well as an ape-like being. Then his focus shifted. "I see myself travelling down a corridor made of metal. They are doing something with energy that I don't understand. This place is made of metal that occasionally looks like it is grown and not made. The metal is transforming its shape into something that is living. That memory is very clear, these images all seem part of myself."

He closed his eyes. I was intrigued and determined to keep everything on track, "Look down and tell me what your body looks like."

"It's dim and bluish grey, there doesn't seem to be any sexual function. It's all there, but it looks like it's not switched on."

"Do you know where your body came from?" I asked.

"It was made, just like the rest of us in this place. Yes, I remember this, I feel very much in that body now. It doesn't have the option to leave if it wants to, it just lies there. It seems very mechanical but I know that it is living. Everything is being changed as we go along, like having three fingers or four fingers. There are no fingernails, but noticing the absence of something is part of the creation. I know things are not going to stay like this very long, I am on an assembly line."

This seemed similar to James' story of being assembled in a gas filled chamber. "What is happening to you?"

"I am, at the moment, being created and whatever else it is that they are doing. I am floating in a womb, resting in that place. Others like me are in this place. There is a strange new feeling that I do not like."

"Are you suffering?"

"Ever so slightly. There is a warm sort of gentle cocoon feeling and I am very safe. But, there is this new unpleasant feeling, what you would call pain. It is a very odd thing this pain."

"What happens to make you feel pain?"

"What they are doing to control the making of the body, the way they are trying to arrange it. There are all these unusual sensations. We are being evolved at some sort of speed. We are people being made by people. This is because we need physical alterations to make inhabiting the surface possible."

At that moment, it all seemed right on track to me. "The people they are making, what are they like?"

"They have this weird fear, these new animals with a lower frequency. It's not like the high and light feeling, the low frequency seems very unusual."

Steven began to squirm nervously in his chair, "I remember a lot of fighting and arguing that had been taking place in a different time altogether. Whoever made the decision to leave the planet said it was for the best. Now I am back here as an ape creature, and maybe that was not such a good idea. With all the genetic engineering problems that went unsolved, I shouldn't be back here."

He was becoming excitable, so I tried changing the subject, "Before you were in this place, do you know where you came from?"

"I do, but it's not with that body at all. It's more like the people with the robes. I am not sure what has happened, I have dissociated from the blue body."

"What is going on now?" I asked him. He became calm and his voice changed into a different tone.

"At the moment I see us dressed up ceremonially in robes. We all come from the same source. Ours is a whole society living in many cities, we have our life styles and jobs. For two or three centuries before we were instructed to leave, there was a spiritual movement to align us with the technology advancement. That is why we are dressed the same for this ceremony, to show that we are united."

"Describe the ceremony that is taking place," I suggested.

"I see the emperor lizard manifesting along with a Draco consciousness as a temporary incarnation just before the ceremony begins. Next to them on a stage, the king lizard and his queen sit with hands resting on the arms of their thrones."

"They wear purple robes that are extremely ornate with gold fringes. The king wears a red cap with gold cascading down the back. The queen sitting next to him wears a little bit of a crown on her head. They are both wearing all sorts of ornaments. They have the languid, self-confident look that your leaders of today have. They move slowly and do not appear respectful of anyone.

"Their long faces taper down. The eyes are somewhat on the side of the head. The large hands have three fingers and a thumb, with long yellowish claws.

"The king has a deep burgundy skin with a golden orange under belly. The queen's skin is a deep blue. The eyes are crystal blue and her body is ever so slightly transparent. There is an almost etheric look about her, as if she is in several dimensions at once. There is a pulse at the side of her neck. Otherwise, she is like a piece of stone. Now she is sort of waking up, moving around a bit. It's as if she is returning from a trance. The blue eyes are changing colour to a brown shade, the colour of regular lizard eyes. While in the astral, her eyes change colour. On returning, she looks just like everyone else. Her blue consciousness seemed to be a combination of entities. A divine spirit used part of her to channel into this place.

"Standing in a symmetrical fashion on either side of the royals are smaller lizard people with blue, yellow, and red skin. Blue skin seems to be important to the lizards. This group moves around a lot and seems to be afraid all the time.

"Another lizard appears to be the queen's sister. Well, not like a birth sister, more like sisters that are discovered to have the power. Next to her is a stiff lizard with blue eyes. Blue eyes indicate the ones that are channelling.

"To one side there is a curtained off area, behind which is a group of the *Draco*. They seem very anxious and walk around in a circle. They are meditating in a group consciousness, trying to invoke someone's presence."

There it was again, the word **Draco**, "Who are the Draco, are they working with the royal lizards?"

"The royals are being filled with instructions from the Draco's, telling them what to do. The Draco's behind the curtain are themselves looking for instructions from the Draco hierarchy. This is interesting, they think something is going to happen, but it is not.

"Seated in the front row of the audience are the dignitaries of the lizard people. Sitting behind them are the military high command. Further on are bureaucrats, officials, and other important people. At the very back, the star people from the mothership are seated. They haven't been given very nice seating, although this is supposed to be a union of the two races.

"Two rather plain looking star people, the commander and his wife, approach the stage. They have standard pale skin bodies, large black eyes, and clarity of perception. As they come up to meet with the royals, the Draco's behind the curtain cloak themselves, because they don't want to be noticed.

"The female star person is communicating telepathically with her husband as they walk towards the royals, 'Are they going to give it to us?' she says. He answers, 'We shall just have to see.'

"I don't really know what this ceremony is for, there are so many conflicting thoughts. Everybody thinks the ceremony is for something different.

"The female star person seems to have been given the impression that the lizard people are going to move out. Wherever she got that information from could not have been a reliable source, because the Draco and the lizard people do not intend to leave Earth. While they are saying the star

Egarina and Alcheringa approach the dais for the Handover Ceremony

people are the new custodians, they have nothing like that in their minds.

"The Draco's have decided the way to stop them is to eat them both, in fact all the star people. But, when several of the cloaked Draco's emerge from behind the curtain, they find it impossible to eat the commander and his wife. This is because they are enveloped in a shield of protection. So, they go ahead with a ceremony.

"There is an exchange with the hands, symbolically passing energy from one to the other. All the lizard people begin to roar, it is truly a disgusting sound. You can tell by the sound of everybody's voice that while they have done the ritual, it doesn't seem to have worked. The star people walk past the lizard people as they depart, wondering where all this is going to lead to.

"There is a ship outside, a large white one. The star people get on it and return to the mothership. The whole ceremony was a big nothing. The royals didn't really know what it was for. These creatures are slimy and devious, but they do as they are told. Nothing had been arranged to carry out a hand-over ceremony. They didn't know where it was supposed to lead to, so they just followed instructions. Through the influence of the Draco, the emperor lizard says to the king lizard, 'Kill them all, and blow up the mothership.'"

Steven's voice shifted into one with an almost diplomatic tone. He introduced himself as **Binjala from the Elohim**, the one who was guiding Steven through the regression.

"When we choose to manifest, our people have large limbs and an almost human-like body. There are different expressions of the face, more divine, I would even say omnipotent. We are exceptionally present, yet other worldly at the same time. Some of us are quite concerned about things, and we are very much into doing. We are into counselling, great strength of body, and manifestation. This is what we do when we have need. We can work simultaneously in over six thousand places in space time, all at once, all over the place.

"You see, we needed a small number of star creatures from the various star systems to come down to the planet, to allow us to work out the details of increasing the general energy of the sphere. We needed an influence from their consciousness to be brought to Earth. We said we could do it without them if they were not willing to give up specimens of themselves to be genetically altered.

"The star people replied that if they were to come to this place, they would bring themselves. We thought this was a poor idea, but it was the way they chose to move. They were quite emphatic about establishing colonisation for their own society. We tried to explain that conditions on the planet would be difficult and extremely hostile. We told them that the chance of their making it in the usual way of colonisation was unlikely. They said this was the way they would keep their civilisation going. We replied, 'There are other ways that you can have your energy dispersed on this planet, you do not have to live here.' They would not listen.

"They seemed to think that their presence was necessary, that it would hold a value to their sense of community, and all the rest of it. They said it was easier to bring families that could adjust to the Earth slowly, rather than us taking them as genetic information.

"So, we sort of let them go that way. We all agreed that it would just be for the benefit of the planet, and that the whole situation would work without a flaw. We gave them assurances that it would be organised and safe. That is what we told them."

He laughed.

"They seemed quite convinced they could make small genetic changes to themselves along the way and get by. We had our doubts. Actually, there were no doubts. We knew the future. We were just being softly polite. They did not have the technology to survive, but off they went."

There was something strange about his laugh.

Steven's head snapped up, and he stared at me with the coldest look. His voice shifted into one with a different, unsatisfying quality about it.

"I present to you the Draco consciousness underlying the lizard emperor. You would not like me, I am quite crocodile in my features. My skin is leathery with little bumps. I have a large, almost dragon-like snout, with many teeth. There are large ears."

He paused and stared at me again. I got nervous, "Yes?"

"Our visit is a great honour for the lizard people, who see us as their gods. Of course they do, we are their creators, their lords and masters who set them free a long time ago. We have since moved on to another dimension through a gateway. We could not care less about what happens to the lizard people, or for any of the other creations we made for that matter. Now we have returned and presented ourselves for the ceremony.

"I'm just looking after Earth for a little while, somebody else will look after it in the future. Hmm, I see myself eat the consciousness of a small ape-like being. I remember feeding off different beings in this place by eating their consciousness."

Eating their consciousness, what kind of creature was this Draco? "How do you feel doing something like that?"

"Well, I don't seem to have a feeling of any sort, there seems to be no real purpose in what we are doing here. Oh! Yes there is! We Draco have come to take the gold that the ape-like creatures mine for us."

"What do you use the gold for?"

Drawing of Draco star people

"It's a transmutational thing. It creates little vortices in our bodies after we ingest it. This white powder gold allows us to manipulate the atoms somewhat. We become more transparent, enabling us to move into another dimension. Just now I am moving through a time-tunnel into a town that looks like somewhere in the USA during the nineteen-thirties. I walk up to some guy, just to see what happens, and he runs off screaming. Oh, I still look like a Draco. I should have changed that image. Running away was the best thing he could do, we Draco can't move very fast.

"You know, just by walking up to someone I can consume all or just part of their consciousness. The person that is in the body doesn't like it at all. No one seems to like it when you walk up and consume him or her. At least none of the people I ate seem to have liked it."

He heaved out a dry cackle.

"That's part of the whole personality of the Draco, the memories of hundreds and thousands of screaming people."

The idea was horrific, "You just take over their bodies?"

"No, in order to live I eat people by consuming their consciousness. I have no concern about their bodies."

"Do you have any feelings about that?"

"I just feel like I have everyone else's feelings. It's hard to find something that isn't an echo of the people I have consumed. It's a different perspective, yet the whole idea seems foreign to me when I look at things that way. I seem to be everybody else's memory and desire to continue."

The regression was getting more unreal by the second, "Are you happy to let that go on?"

"Well, I don't think I am happy, but I am not particularly disturbed by it. You see, it is just what I do. It never occurred to me to wonder about doing something different. I am sure I would die if I stopped."

"Does that worry you?"

"The idea of dying? Yes it actually does. There would be a sense of horror, a sort of drifting into the centre of all the feelings of the people I have consumed. If I were to die it would mean that, well, I would literally fall in amongst them."

This was out of a horror movie; "You sound like Dracula."

He roared with laughter, "That word comes from Draco."

That would make sense, "Are there others like you?"

"Like me who feed off people? Oh yes, lots! That is what we all do. And do you know what? We Draco live an exceptionally long time."

"Are there any races superior to you?"

"There are conscious beings that we are unable to consume, expansive crystalline structures. This doesn't normally happen, I mean usually we just walk up to something and eat it, and there is no tactic, no real process."

He shook his head, "Anyway, when we stand in front of these things, their consciousness seems much larger than ours. We have some awe concerning these crystalline structures. We don't have much capacity for that kind of feeling, but there is a sense of it."

"Describe them", I suggested.

"Okay, I'll try to go down deep inside the consciousness of the Draco, past all these traumatised people."

Steven's voice returned to normal.

"This is odd. I can see a crystal within a golden coloured cylinder arrangement. This is being held in place by a crystalline body structure. The hands have a sensor like quality."

Steven struggled to speak, and then the Draco voice returned.

"Cradled within the cylinder is a crystal filled with light. It gives me the impression that it's an agent of the angelic, as if they were involved in its construction. The innate depth of darkness within the Draco is contradictory to that. Yet, there is some sense of longing towards the angelic realms.

"The sense of lightness seems quite attractive, but the depth of the memory of suffering is so vast, well, it seems an impossible task. I see no way to move in order to make that start happening. There doesn't seem to be a gateway for us to change what we do. Our lives are so simple, so straight forward, it seems so necessary that we keep plodding on.

"You see, many millions of years ago, the passage of people on a particular Draconian ship became significant. In passing through a dimensional sea, we found an interesting energy for the Draco to feed off. It is rather like bait in a way, you put out a flower and we come to it like a bee. We were able to alter some of the details of the matrix formation of our energy group to allow us to feed our own machinery, our own processes, and all the various works that we are involved in. So in exchange for the donation of their energy for our machinery, we integrate it. They all seem to think we are just taking from them, plugging into their consciousness and using their power. Yet, there is a perfect balance of energy. We give the same amount of Draco energy back in exchange.

"The Draco energy has been useful in mirroring the consciousness of a planet, a sole entity incarnated with myriad forms of itself. This creates quite a powerful crystalline geometric structure for a planet."

"Imagine a dying planet with one billion people and say only a million souls, all incarnated at once, that's a thousand bodies for each soul. The fewer the number of souls, the more bodies each soul occupies. This is like a nuclear reactor of energy, perfectly radiant. The soul geometry of a planet becomes quite spectacular and refines the energy of the planet. So, on that last day of inhabitation, there are say a billion bodies and only one soul. When that last soul leaves, the entire population dies in an instant. At that moment the planet becomes aware of itself.

"The last energy the planet encounters is a singular consciousness. That energy, that consciousness, is passed on to the planet, something we Draco like immensely, for it is a useful ally to us."

I didn't understand any of that, and I looked at him with a furrowed brow, "Do the Draco exist here in our time?"

"Not in this particular place. I mean, we have been here in the past and will be again in the future, but we are not here at the moment."

That was certainly a relief, "Are the Reptoids like you?"

"The lizards are more brain oriented. They move and act quicker, responding to each other in a more intense way. They are male and female, and they have a lot of aggression. The one I control, the king lizard, is very much interested in power. He views the situation in terms of his personal power and prestige. He seeks to aggress himself over others, physically or otherwise, for he always ..."

Steven paused for a long beat. When he began to speak again, his voice sounded normal.

"That is what was odd. While painting on a section of the fresco, I remembered working on the hieroglyphs. I remembered another wall, one where I wasn't working with a brush. I was cutting with a piece of metal that was running out of energy and fading away. I started using a little tool, and then that became damaged, so I picked up a rock and kept on going. I ran out of energy and was given divine instruction to go to another place. There I was pulled out of the trauma of the old memory. I was evolved into an improved life form, making it more like what I really came for."

Steven opened his big blue eyes and sat upright with a bright smile, his young face a picture of innocence.

The next revelation came in the form of Michael.

Michael independently visited the site at Kariong. Within the first fifteen minutes of seeing the hieroglyphs, he was over-whelmed with confusing emotions and images in his mind. Somebody gave him my phone number. When he eventually rang, I arranged for him to visit.

Michael induced conflicting emotions within me from the second I opened the front door. I usually get an immediate reaction to people, either positive or negative, but with Michael, I seemed to have both.

He eventually settled into the hot seat with the photos, and I coaxed him into a starship memory while describing the two scout ships landing at Kariong. In his memory, he per-ceived two angels holding his hands, taking him towards the mother ship. When I tried to direct him onto the ship he had difficulty seeing himself there, and began to speak with some hesitation.

"I see a reptile form, I can feel hands with webbed fingers, it's not right."

"Where do you see yourself?"

"I'm on another ship, something's wrong."

His pupils were open wide in the light filled room. His hands began shaking, so I tried to reassure him, "That's okay, just go along with the images. Focus a little more and ask the angels what it is that they want you to understand."

He calmed a bit, so I tentatively dived in, "What does the reptile form look like?"

"He has slits for eyes, very piercing yellow humanoid eyes. There is sort of a scaly mane going over the back of his head and some scraggly hair in the front. He is wearing a slip-over thing with yellow coloured sleeves. He has arms and legs, and a tail extending out the back. His head is in reasonable proportion to the rest of the body, but he is clearly reptile."

"I know that I am here, but at the same time feel that I am there. I am not actually in that body, but I am experiencing those feelings. I feel anger towards that scaly person, yet I am just an observer."

Michael frowned, "No, it is more than that. He is looking out of the window of a ship. I think he is some sort of a commander. Now he is giving an order to fire on the ship, he wants me to destroy it. Oh no, now I am firing a particle beam weapon into the star ship."

To my horror, he seemed to be the Reptoid who actually shot the mother ship out of the sky. Michael was yelling while at the same time I felt indignant, "Do you feel good about that?" His voice then became very soft, "No, a part of me hurts. I am that being."

He sobbed openly, releasing an ancient guilt. For a moment, I did not know what to do. Inside I felt a mixture of sympathy and anger. Then I realised that he was experiencing

Drawing of a Reptoid wearing the robe of a chamberlain

karma the same as me, just as Egarina had explained. "Michael, I can see that you are hurting, please don't judge yourself."

He shook his head vigorously, "No, there is a huge mushroom shaped ship in the process of exploding, with hundreds of smaller ships flying away from it. Parts of it are beginning to fall down towards the planet. Scout ships are trying to get away, but our ships fire upon them and they just disintegrate. This is inhuman."

He realised that his last remark told the whole story and he laughed bitterly. He was desperately angry with the Reptoid who gave the order, but could find no validity in his anger. He was the one that fired the weapon. A distant aspect of himself had come back nine hundred thousand years later to be faced.

I asked in a cool voice, "What about the scout ships that survived?"

"Teams went down to the planet to search out and destroy them, the last evidence of what we had done. They didn't succeed because they simply couldn't find them. Instead, they took all of the equipment that the star people had off loaded onto the surface of the planet. That was needed for our work. They had killed almost all of the star people, so they just left. The same commander who gave the order to fire ordered them to leave."

"Where did they go?"

"They went back to their command ship. Later on, the ship sort of jumped into another space, and went back to Orion."

Michael began to clutch at his groin, "I feel an awful pain in my stomach, as if I was stabbed with something. Oh, I've been shot by the Reptoids. Maybe I'm not really from Orion. I think I was on the starship. Yes, please let me be from the starship."

His visions were jumping all over the place, as if he had actually been on the mothership as well. This was very confusing.

"No, the Reptoid is part of me. I feel like I was the one giving the order to destroy the starship, even though I know I was standing next to the commander.

"Now I'm down on the surface and feel like I can't breathe. Then I see a different type of Reptoid with horrible red and black mottled skin. He has these terrible red eyes. He has a holster with some sort of a device in it. He takes it out, points it at me, and I fall to the ground. Something hot has gone into my stomach."

Michael began to panic as if he really was shot. I tried to calm him, "Look down at your arms and hands. Describe what they look like."

He seemed surprised, "They're human hands with five fingers, but the arms are dark and scaly."

"Is this how you looked on the ship?"

"It's hard to tell because I have a uniform on. It's a reddish brown colour with yellow sleeves and an insignia on the right arm.

"I remember coming through the planet's atmosphere in a ship and then running for cover. That's when they came and shot me. This is strange, it's like I'm in two places at once. I don't feel good. I have a feeling of unworthiness. It's all mixed up, with the starship being blown apart and then my ship landing. Some people are being injured, and I am shot.

"I have two different feet. One foot is webbed, and the other foot belongs to a star person. It's like I am in two people at once, this is very confusing."

I asked him to let go of the part of him that felt unworthy. He began to calm down, but still appeared as if he couldn't breathe, a reaction that I deeply understood.

"The atmosphere is very sticky. I think I remember being a star person that came down to the planet in a scout ship. The one that broke in half and went into the water."

Then he looked up at me with clear calm eyes, "No, I know who I am."

His voice became very soft as a tear ran down his cheek, "I play the part of a good guy and a bad guy. This allows me to see both sides of the same coin, and the lack of compassion between some. This is my lesson, to understand sorrow so that I can feel compassion and then love."

He smiled at me, "Thank you so much for your help." Then Michael stood up and walked out the front door.

We had a gathering at Alcheringa on a Sunday, an open invitation to friends and neighbours to join us and relax at an informal picnic. As the day wore on, many came and went. One of the visitors, Joseph, talked to me. In his eyes, I saw what looked like an incredible feeling of love that seemed to radiate towards me. I was taken aback as I barely knew this man, but I did recognise he had something to tell me.

I sat with him in my study, showed him the photos of Kariong, the Alcheringa stone sitting nearby, and he recalled memories from the distant past. Joseph seemed quite calm at first, but then so did I.

"Uh, Earth is off to the left. The commander is standing behind me. I am sitting down at a circular panel with a window in front. I think someone is sitting to my right. I feel the curvature of the Earth. I have the feeling of a fleet of ships."

"Turn around and look at the commander behind you, see if you can describe him."

"He is a deep dull red, and reptile."

The hair on the back of my neck stood up, "Red and reptile?"

"Yes, he is in charge."

"Describe his uniform?"

"It's a reddish brown colour with yellow sleeves and an insignia on the right arm."

I thought about Michael's reading. Here was correspondence that was both clear and confusing at the same time. Maybe everyone dressed that way, "How are you dressed?"

"I am the particle beam operator, my uniform is a silvery colour."

Okay, perhaps there were two of them, "The commander is talking to you. What does he tell you?"

"Shoot"

"What? He says shoot?"

Joseph nodded emphatically, "He says shoot, shoot"

An eerie feeling came over me, "Can you see what you are shooting at?"

Minutes went by with nothing being said. "Keep talking," I suggested.

"I see space with the curvature of Earth. I have the sense of many little button shaped craft taking off from a huge ship. There is an explosion or something, an immense explosion."

Anger began to arise in me, "How do you feel about that?"

"Not good"

"Why not?'

"Because I did it."

Here I began to yell a bit, "You did it, why did you do it?"

Joseph's hands began to shake, "My commander told me to shoot, he told me to fire and so I did. There is a light burst that moves with great speed, like a nuclear fission that happens with incredible intensity.

"The ray that is projected is a sound that entrains, I understand this very well. It entrains to a frequency that is similar to the composition of the material that it is destroying, a similar vibration at much higher amplitude that causes it to shatter, just like a singer with a high note shattering a glass."

I felt repulsed with every fibre of my being, but I knew I had to continue. "Go back further in your memory to find out why you are up there, how you got there."

"We came from inner Earth – there is an immense military outpost where we fly out of. I am watching these craft fly out from a deep cavern within the Earth. This is indeed an act of treachery that we are undertaking."

"Why do you think it is treacherous if you are military?"

"Because there is an agreement that these people and their ship are to come in safety. This is treacherous." Joseph broke down and cried. My anger melted away.

"This is a dreadful thing we are doing, we are not evil. I know what I am doing, and at the same time, I know it is wrong. I am trapped in this situation, but I have to go ahead with the act, knowing I should not. Because I am in the military, I have to take orders. You can't get away from it. Because if you ..."

Joseph breathed heavily as he tried to stop crying. A few more minutes went by with nothing being said. I gently touched his shoulder, "What would have happened if you tried to go against the order?"

"They would destroy me instantly."

"How would they destroy you?"

"With light, it can be done with the eyes, they can do it with vision."

"With vision? Are these lizard people with the vision, or are they Draco?"

Joseph shook his head, "I don't know."

"Let's go back before that treacherous act. Did you ever meet some of the people off the starship?"

He seemed confused, "What ship?"

I suddenly felt impatient, "The mothership, the one with the people who came with love. Did you meet them somewhere, like on the ground?"

"No, a meeting is held with the supreme ... I can't remember the name, but it is agreed that this thing is out of control and has to end. We will go away and leave them in peace to inherit the Earth. This is being decreed, there are people wearing purple cloaks."

Here was correspondence with Steven's reading, "Are they lizard people?"

"Yes, they are."

"Are the lizard people in cloaks telling you it's time to leave?"

"Yes. Very long ago, many of us were involved in genetic engineering. Things had got so far out of control that there were giant creatures roaming the Earth, and the planet had become a very unsafe place. This was a power thing that just exploded and became endless.

"They were all trying to out-do each other, trying to be bigger and better. This competition came out of power and greed. They were cross-breeding like boys with big toys, very masculine. There was a total disregard for life."

I calmed down a bit, "Do you know who they make the agreement with?"

"They are pale blue. There is something about these people, a translucency that is in total contrast to the dense physicality of the reptile people into which I am born. They have a lightness or fineness. They almost seem to fly when they move. They are incredibly soft and gentle.

"There is an agreement that the reptile races will actually leave. But they are full of cunning and treachery, and they renege on the agreement. They said they would leave but they do not, they are still here today."

"Where?"

"In the inner Earth."

"Have they changed their ways?"

"No."

This was territory that I did not want to be in. "Let's go back to where you use your particle weapon on the mothership. You see some of the smaller ships getting away. Are you aware of what happens, is there an order to pursue them?"

"Yes there is. Because I hesitate when I fire, my commander orders me to pursue two ships that go towards the south. I enter into a small button shaped craft that leaves the command ship. I take off in pursuit, and can see them ahead of me.

"It is a fine day and there are nice puffy white clouds. One of their ships crashes into the water. Another one is landing safely. I think all the rest of the escaping ships are destroyed."

"Do you try and destroy the remaining ship?"

"No, this is an act of treachery, there is no way these people can defend themselves. I want to find some other alternative. This is before I become aware and turn towards God. Something awakens in me, but I don't know what it is.

"I was present at their first diplomatic meeting on the Earth, and I have the memory of the softness and gentleness of these people. I am drawn to that softness. I have some identity with these people. I am in a state of distress over what I have done, about what I have been told to do. I call on my mother's form of deity to seek his punishment. I seek, I don't know."

Joseph paused for a moment to regain his composure.

"Maybe they are all going to die, but I just want to help them. I decide to desert, feeling that I am meant to follow these people.

"My ship descends vertically to a clearing near bushes and large rocks. I get out and move through the bush to the waters edge, because I am drawn to the blue. As I gaze across the water and the beach, I see Rosalyn for the first time."

That remark was a big surprise. Rosalyn is Joseph's wife in this life.

"I find her on the beach, and all I feel is her softness. Her skin is translucent, she is so gentle. You see, when you are only with your own people, that is all you know. But to suddenly see this other thing, this soft femininity, that is something new.

"She is injured and I want to help her. I have a sense of comforting her, but I don't know what to do. She is just barely conscious and in a state of shock, but she can see me. She accepts me, knowing that I look so different. Because she feels my concern, she is not afraid. It's a bit like the beauty and the beast. I am scaly with a tail and long claws. If I put my hands out to touch her I might hurt her, she is so delicate. I have this clumsiness about me, but it is a kindly clumsiness.

"Two others emerge from the water, wounded and in a state of shock. I sense the presence of another person and turn to see him. He is one of our ape creatures. He has dark skin with curly hair covering his tall body. He is carrying something, perhaps a spear. He comes out from the bush and watches fascinated as the pale blue skinned people walk from the water.

"Then the sun emerges from behind the clouds and the blue people begin to scream in pain." He lowered his head and was silent for a moment.

"I have to learn the right way to go to the light, that is the next evolutionary step. The way I have known life before this moment is very self-centred, you do everything for yourself with disregard for others generally. This is a problem for our society. I am in the military and when we are put together, if we do not work as a team, we are simply destroyed. This is a way of keeping order that is a necessity with us. Suddenly I find myself seeing the explosion, taking off in a craft in pursuit, and then defecting when I find the star people.

"I feel a concern for their wellbeing, and at the same time know that I created their trauma. This is a different way of being, more than just focusing in on myself. For me it is something very new, like a flowering.

"These people have a group consciousness, they are all tuned in to the needs of each other. There is no separation into individuality as in my society. They accept me and give their forgiveness for what I have done. I do my best to help them survive in this terrible situation. For doing this, they give me their love, something quite unlike anything I have ever known.

"They must take their food from the Earth. I am able to help the star people become aware of plants that are dangerous to them because of their molecular vibrations, yet I can do nothing to protect them against the bacteria and insects that ravage their sensitive bodies. Affection develops between Rosalyn and me. She helps me just by being what she is. The more that I develop, the more I learn about quality of life, affection, and being sincere.

"I have changed, my claws aren't as pointed or talon-like as they were. This means that I can touch these people. I love to feel the softness of their skin, the incredible softness.

"The star people realise that the only way they can continue as a people on the Earth is to inter-breed with an existing species that is able to thrive here. They choose the little hairy ones, a species we ourselves created."

Now I understood why the survivors of the Rexegena inter-bred with the ape creature.

"In the new ones, the bone density has to increase to take the atmospheric pressure, and to be physically strong enough to live on the Earth. The star people come from an atmosphere that is vastly different, and their bodies are much softer. Their offspring have to solidify more. Their skin cannot take exposure to the sun's rays, so the substance of their flesh has to alter. Yes, there is a reconfiguration needed. I take some blood samples from the hairy ones. Some conversion is done and the samples are placed into the star people."

"What are the particulars of the inter-breeding?"

"It occurs at the molecular level."

"Do you mean DNA?"

"That feels very right yes, but you see I am not around anymore because they come and get me."

"Get you? Who comes and gets you?"

"My own commander comes after me, he destroys me."

"What about the star people?"

"He just leaves them there."

"Do you know why he just leaves them?"

"No, I am dead."

Joseph opened his eyes and viewed me sadly.

These three regressions made me realise how important it is not to judge anyone. We all live out different roles in various bodies, both here on Earth and in the cosmic worlds. In our collective experience, we will all eventually come to understand compassion and love.

Steven saw the Draco who commanded the lizard king to destroy the star people. Michael saw the Reptoid commander who gave the order to shoot the mothership. Joseph saw the particle beam operator who finally destroyed it. These are nice friendly people who had never met. Each had come to me to recall memories that linked together in perfect order.

In some ways, I feel a little mixed up, and there is still anger inside me. But now I have a greater understanding of how things work, and life is not as simple as it was before. It would seem that the purpose of much of the human race is to give those who live out lives in Draco, Reptoid, and Dinoid cultures an opportunity to live out lives as humans. We are a different kind of being in this part of the galaxy, one with a built-in understanding of love and compassion.

The people come forward, it's like they each have a number. Egarina reminds me, "Your availability is important, do not get caught up in other work."

Looking like a Reptoid

CHAPTER 7

Robbie's Regression
Alcheringa talks about the end
of the Rexegena
Glenda's Regression

Robbie frowned, "We are not in the right place."

"Where should we be then?" I replied.

"Not here, we are not ready. I can't see this working at all. No one in this group is aligned to my vibration and the way I work. I am not sure how I am going to be able to encode on my own."

Her terms were a bit confusing to me, "Are you drawing from this or another time?"

"Another time. I am very anxious. I can't see survival in this place. There simply aren't enough of us. There should be eight of my vibration."

"What happened to the others of your vibration?"

"They were just blown away, it was all very sudden. I don't know why I am here with these people, their origins are different."

"How are you different? Look at your hands, tell me what you see."

Robbie started to hum as she looked from side to side with eyes closed tight, "Hmm, these are my sensors yes. There are circles on the hands with four crystalline fingers."

Steven's description of the crystalline consciousness inside a cylinder loomed up in my mind, "Are you a crystal consciousness in a golden cylinder, like a kind of crystalline robot?"

"Yes, a group of us work telepathically to bring in the knowledge and the information. We cannot work with the other people in the same way, they just don't have the alignment."

"Where do you obtain this knowledge?"

"The information is from the Elohim, they are my origin. Something has happened. I don't know why I am on this scout ship. I am meant to be with my own kind, but these people asked me at the last moment.

"Our ship has come in, but it's the only ship that has survived. I do not see the point in being here, it hasn't been revealed to me yet. All the people are coming to me wanting to know. I am the radio or the transmitter of the frequency. They don't know how to survive here, and they feel I can make something happen. I do not have the knowledge they seek. It is not what I do. What I have is the vibration to help them do what they do.

"My role is to bring about harmony, to bring in the high frequency. This is because I can receive and transmit that very easily. This tone will bring everyone into balance quickly.

"They are very worried, but I have to separate. I can't attune when I am being bombarded with information. The feeling of fear and the questions create a situation in which I cannot function. I need to be separate to align with the vibration, to bring it through so that it can penetrate the group. This is a big job, because I am the only one here of my alignment.

"There is some danger here and survival is the first issue. Nobody knows if we can survive in this place. There is a way of purifying the water, they cannot drink the water. The Elohim are showing me how the water contains microbes that the beings from the ship cannot handle. They must not touch the water as it is. It is too hot for my mechanism. I cannot function in the heat, my origins are cool.

"These people, their fear of surviving, the wanting to get everything under control, it makes me feel like I am choking. A calmness and inner peace is what I need. I must concentrate, yet I cannot find the space. I am a long way from home, but I know what is happening. I must ask the others to be quiet, to leave me alone so that I can bring in the information.

"To submerge me in fear and emotion cuts off the connection. Some in the group have very strong involvement with information. Sorting and shifting through information is their role, and that is the very thing that cuts me off, it comes as a bombardment. I need to discern where I can best be of service to the overall, but there is also a need to survive. How else can I protect them?"

Another part of Steven's regression came to mind, "Did you and the others of your group protect the star people at the changeover ceremony?"

"One of our roles is that of detector, a detector of anything that takes away from the higher frequency. Anything that lowers that frequency triggers a safety mechanism, because ultimately that frequency would cause the star people not to be able to function."

Robbie's mood shifted for just an instant, "We know the Draco and their hunger, but it's a bit like putting human beings under water and expecting them to be happy where they cannot breathe."

Robbie's face returned to worry, "The Elohim are telling me that there must be procreation, the survival of these people depends on it. But this cannot simply be from within the group, it must come from outside. They must find the highest evolved on this planet, and bring about children in combination with their species.

"As I bring in this information, there is a lot of talk. It is very hard to get them to understand that I can only function in silence, because I am picking up vibrations that come from far away. The Elohim will provide the knowledge, they will make a species available and provide, step by step, what is needed for this mission to be successful.

"The star people are saying, 'Tell them to come and take us away.' They are all asking questions, and there is fear coming in from them. I say, 'Stand back, stand back, your role is yet to come, my role is to tell you. There are beings in the group who have the knowledge to bring about procreation.' In their calmness they will remember, they will know what to do instead of being caught up in this vibration of fear.

"It is a big task to get them to settle. They want me to give them visions of the future to reassure them, their telepathic abilities are not as strong. I give each one visions in the night to encourage them. The Elohim say they will empower them. I worry that I will be enough for the task, it seems so enormous.

"The star people all have different origins. Each raises questions, which raises more questions. I am finding it necessary to detach from the questions and simply go within, that is where I get my rest.

"Much of what they are discussing I do not know, that is their area of expertise. Someone is talking about food. Someone else is talking about water to drink, and how they can make it safe. He was given symbols in his dreams and now he remembers, so I can stand back saying nothing. Things are starting to change. All are being worked with telepathically and starting to remember their roles.

"I bring in the energy of the Elohim to help imprint them with what they need to do. This is the beginning and they are not yet adjusted to where they are. The presence of the Elohim ray makes it much easier for me now, because I can function.

"I am more stabilised in who I am and this resonates with the others, they too are empowered by that ray. This is my role. The group's ability is wonderful.

"The people question why it is not possible to send more of us. I tell them it's an enormous task, but one that must be done. Once it begins more will come, they are not needed at this time. They do not understand that their species are easily influenced by the vibrational pull of this planet. They cannot see what is happening. I myself can see it because my attunement is finer, and when something comes along that is not of the higher vibration, I feel it immediately.

"I can sense the density and the frequency of the planet permeating them. This is possibly a natural occurrence. I don't know whether to allow the saturation of this frequency in myself, or to maintain my origins. This is my dilemma. Will it work best if I become one of them and reconnect, or should I maintain my identity and my sense of separation? I am not sure, but I will do whatever serves the overall good. I am in a quandary, but it is apparently my own decision. What do I do here?

"I am shown these funny looking people who look like tall bears. They are friendly, but they have a very low frequency."

"Why do you say they look like bears?"

"They are strong, hairy, and very dense. There is no compatibility. I don't see how they are going to do this."

"Do what?" I asked.

"There is the need for a connection with this species in order to ensure survival into the future. The doctors have remembered what they can do to impregnate these beasts. I don't see how this will be possible, but that is the information the Elohim have given me. I must go with what I am told, what I know to be right.

"It seems that I will be here for a very long time. I must serve where I can, and take time out when I need to. Each one must find their way. I cannot take on responsibility for everybody. This is difficult as I can see they are having dilemmas, and I know that by settling their vibrations they will come to know. I must detach from even this to maintain the link over a long period of time.

"Many things are being shown to me so that I can understand. I am forward in time, and there are babies about to be born. My role here is to encode each one of the souls coming through with the frequency of the Elohim, to be awakened at a much later time."

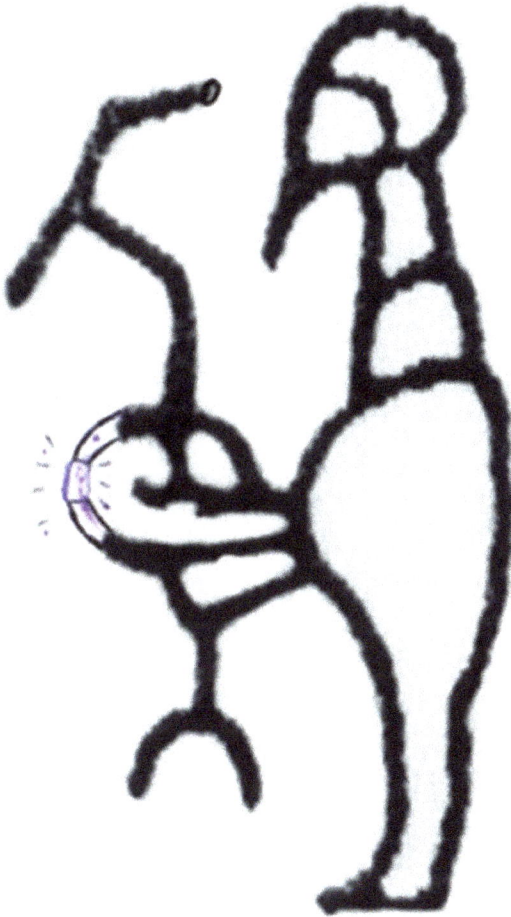

Enlarged hieroglyph at Kariong

Here, a crystal "robot" is energising the foetus of a new race in the pregnant star-lady. What looks like a head on her is actually similar to a telephonic communication connected to her helmet which functions to keep disruptive energies away. The "sparkles" on the robot (on the left side) are actually energy emanating from the crystal (energising the foetus).

"I will be connected with this species down through time, and I will reconnect with them when this planet goes through its evolutionary shift. I will awaken the memory within their hearts, the memory of who they are. Yet, they are coming from the beasts, and I am very concerned about the outcome. I have been reassured by the Elohim, but I am not certain."

Tears ran down Robbie's face.

"Many of these souls are known to me, and I will be connected with them to the end of this planet. I will have to reconnect with them at various stages of their growth, through many life spans. I am told that this will work, but I am not sure.

"While implanting the vibration, I am assured that it will sustain them. You think that it will, but you never quite know. There are many of us meant to be here, yet there are so few. All my comfort and connection comes from those that are not here, I am so different."

"Do you trust what the Elohim are telling you?"

Robbie was silent for what seemed like a long time. A thousand emotions crossed her face, "I have no knowledge of their expertise, and I only have their assurance that it will be all right. What I need is to hold this first child with my sensors, to feel its vibrational frequency, and to know."

I asked her to move forward in her memory to the point where she was holding a child.

Robbie smiled, "They are all right, and I am able to telepathically communicate with each one. They are ape people – strong but with a soft heart."

"Who are their mothers?"

"There are different lots because they are trying to find the right combination. Some are mothered by the star people, others are by the hairy people."

"Are the children birthed by the star people different from the children of the hairy people? Are they more intelligent?"

"I don't have that information, I only work in the way that I do. I have communication with everyone, but I do not know. It is not necessary."

"Move along until it is time for you to leave the Earth," I suggested.

"The communication with the Elohim is not as clear as it was in the beginning and is getting more difficult. I am between two worlds now, not in my world, and not of this one. My mechanism is getting very old, and I don't know how long I can keep working at this rate. The vibration of this planet takes from me very quickly, and I must replenish my energy."

"Are you worried?"

"I still don't know if they will be all right. There is a gentleness and sensitivity within their hearts, but there is also harshness in this world. I am not sure how they will come to terms with the gentleness inside and the harshness outside. Now I must leave, I cannot stay any longer. There are others coming, they are showing me the future."

Robbie smiled and sighed deeply, "This is the source, such light, such love and joy. The council is pleased with what has taken place. There are concerns, but they are still very pleased with the outcome. Now others will come.

"It was difficult and seemed to take so very long. They are trying to help me work through that. They are showing me family trees from the beginning to this time, the transitions, and the reality. The trees have little faces all over them. They show me that, as time moves on, things change and are different. They tell me to lighten up, let it go, for all is well."

Robbie opened her eyes and looked at me, "Yes, all is well."

I smiled at her, "Do you feel better now?"

"Most definitely, now I have insight into the enormous sense of responsibility I have felt all my life."

Robbie's regression left me with the feeling of being the communicator who somehow failed to bring her communication crystal to Earth, leaving everyone cut off from home base. Why didn't I bring it?

I needed Alcheringa to help me with the memory, so I called his name.

"Good morning my dear, I am very pleased that you have called upon me. I very much miss speaking to you, and I would like to speak to you of these things. I hope you will call upon me more often."

It had been some time, "Yes of course, Alcheringa. I'm sorry I haven't been communicating. I am always thinking of you. I wonder if you can help me. I would like to talk about the time when the mothership blew up. I know it happened very quickly. Can you tell me what happened to the communication crystal, why didn't I, as Egarina, bring it?" Alcheringa seemed to sense the wavering in my voice that betrayed my emotions.

"My dear, you must accept the fact that there was no time to do anything other than hurry to the nearest lifeboat. When the ship began to shudder and explode, there was no time to get anything at all. In fact, you had no time to collect your children or your husband."

"You were in another part of the mothership, and were drawn very quickly to get into the closest lifeboat. There was knowingness in all of what was going to happen, and so you moved quickly. You had great apprehension about your loved ones, and of course, the crystal."

"How did Robbie come to be on the lifeboat?"

"In moving to the lifeboat, you came across one of the crystal robots. You had the presence of mind to ask the robot to come with you, as your instinct knew it would be necessary, for you could see in your mind what was happening to the mother ship."

Intensely bright colours flashed across my vision, and there was a loud ringing in my ears. I felt as if some memory was being played out for me.

"You are now recalling a dream you had many years ago when you saw the mothership exploding. It was as if there was a nuclear reaction, and in some ways, there was. This is the memory you saw in your dream. There are many colours present, but the ultra-violet blue light in particular is what you remember. Can you see how sudden it all was?"

"Yes," I said, remembering the colour of that tragic blue light. A mixture of anxiety and profound sadness enveloped me.

"This is indeed what happened. Once again, you experience the deep anxiety you felt as the two little ships headed towards the planet Earth. But you must understand that you did succeed in what you went there to do. You had the presence of mind to bring the robot with you. The crystalline being within the robot assisted you to maintain a certain frequency of consciousness. The consciousness of all the survivors was lowered once you entered the frequency that existed on Earth. The robot enabled all of you to free yourselves of the anxiety and trauma, and to be able to communicate telepathically with each other."

"Could you please explain what a crystalline robot is?"

"Yes, this being was an **Ishnaan**. The Ishnaans came from a slightly different dimension. These beings, which were actually crystalline, were able to move and have physical presence in the robot form that you mention. They existed in the fifth/sixth dimensions, and gave of themselves to assist the many races of the physical universe. A being from these dimensions became part of the structure of a crystal, and operated their consciousness through that.

"This was at a time when an edict of the Elohim allowed this evolution to take place. It was the joining of an angelic presence into a crystalline substance. These beings were allowed to evolve into another consciousness. The crystal can also be associated with the world of magic. In other words, it is connected with a point of no limit. It is connected with manifestation. It is connected with creation itself."

"Will humans in their evolution ever catch up to that?"

"The crystal, or Christ consciousness, has not evolved in the human to the extent that others in the cosmic worlds have. That is the difference. Because they are in your future, you will never catch up to them.

"To move on to the angelic way of being is to have the magic that goes with it. This will not take place until the beings that will live in the golden age leave their bodies. It will only take place with those that have developed and understand their crystalline energy, their Christ energy, their angelic being.

"God is the source of creation, and the creator of all. It is a love force, and no form takes life without the presence of God. Sometimes individual energies within the love force get confused and pull away from this knowledge. This is the case with those who created the Draco, who in turn created the reptilian races, who in turn created the little hairy upstanding ape on the Earth. These are races that were created

without love, and do not understand it. That is why they are here on the Earth, to learn to understand in a physical body that is imbued with love.

"This knowledge has been called the Christ consciousness, but it is actually the crystal consciousness. It is the angelic presence within all. This has been a little misunderstood down through the ages, but it is well understood in the cosmic worlds.

Evolution will continue in the Earth dimension, and there will be a moving of the earthling into the golden age, which will be one of no limit. Then there will be an understanding of always coming to agreement, respecting each other in different points of view, in a place where love and compassion will prevail."

"Yes, Alcheringa, thank you very much."

There was a long moment of silence, as if Alcheringa were watching me.

"Be at peace my dear, all is well."

The feeling of his presence left me.

I sat quietly in my study and contemplated. In one of their regressions, James and Tricia remembered sitting with me as their mother while I was wearing the crystal on my head. Tricia said it was kept in the same box she sat on as a young girl, the one in the command room at the time we were moving from one dimension into another.

I don't know why, but I rang them to see if they could remember the colour of the crystal. It seemed important to me at that moment. James came back with the answer immediately.

His voice was soothing, and it calmed me, "Your head, as a star woman, sloped back from the brow, allowing the crystal to sit comfortably. The crystal was a very pale fluorescent green colour, almost clear. When activated by your mind it became a different colour, changing relative to what you were doing and with whom you were communicating. The colours were the pale ones seen in mother of pearl, or moonstone.

"You had the ability to project your spirit into this crystal, to activate or amplify all the facets. You had insight into every aspect of the prism, for you were in a divine state in that dimension.

"The Communication Crystal was lost in the destruction of the mothership. Had you attempted to retrieve it, you would have died along with the others. What would have been the sense in that?"

I hung up the phone agreeing with him. It seemed pointless going on about this thing. I felt better, as if a heavy weight had been lifted from my heart.

My sister-in-law, Glenda, had been very interested in the hieroglyphs right from the beginning. When I told her what James had said to me, she began to get upset on the phone. I suggested that we get together and try a regression.

The day loomed cloudy and very wet as Glenda held the pictures of the hieroglyphs. Her experience in meditation led her quickly into an alpha state.

"There is a feeling of falling from a great height into the water, yet I have no fear of drowning. The water is clear, bubbly, and green. I float up to this beautiful face, a sea lion with little whiskers and the most beautiful round compassionate eyes. I'll never forget that face. I can't seem to move very well as I have been injured."

"Why do you say that?"

"Well, I am sort of numb, but I don't feel any pain. There are other sea lions around, and they push me through the water into what seems like a little horseshoe of rock. They nudge me onto my back so that my head and shoulders are supported by the rock. The rest of my body lies in a shallow pool of water at the shore, perhaps to protect me from the sun, I don't know. I have the feeling of being male. I also feel as if I am waiting there because I know the others are coming."

"Is there someone else around?"

"No, this little sea lion face fills my entire vision."

"For a moment, go back before you were in the water and tell me what was happening."

Glenda broke down and began to sob, "I feel an incredible anguish."

I tried to reassure her, "It's just a memory, so don't be afraid, just let it out. Tell me why you feel this way."

Glenda fought to speak as the sobbing wracked her body, "My body is having a hard time because it doesn't want to feel this again. It's just so dreadful."

"It's okay. All this was a long time ago. Please tell me what it is that you are so anguished about."

"It's all gone wrong. The mission, how could this happen? This experience is unbelievable."

"What is happening?"

"From out of nowhere there is destruction."

"What are you doing before the destruction takes place?"

"I'm rejoicing because we are nearly there. It is so thrilling because all our plans are coming to completion. We are all looking at this beautiful place, so blue and green, scintillating like a jewel. There is a feeling of great peace and stillness as we float in space with this beautiful vision filling our sight. Everybody is entranced by this place. We aren't paying attention to anything else because there doesn't seem to be any need. We are safe. Everything is as it should be."

"What happens then?"

"Everybody is frozen in disbelief, something has hit the mothership. We all return to our stations, and the children are gathered up. There is an emergency, sound of a bell, then an evacuation. I hear a roaring sound, like the sound of a huge wave that is gathering to break.

"I feel as if I know what is going to happen, and there is nothing I can do to stop it. I am trying to focus on my training, what I am supposed to do."

"What are you supposed to do?"

"I have to take something. Now I am in a little craft, it's only for one person, like a little pod. It seems to have a cargo that is important to us. They seem to glow, they are crystals."

"Are these to do with communication?"

"Partly, but not completely, most of the crystals help us to anchor the God energy. There is one clear blue-green crystal that is so beautiful, faceted the way a diamond is. That one is for communication. I climb into the pod with just the crystals. There is no time to get anything else. I am holding in my mind that I need to be in front of the energy that is coming to sweep me away. If I worry about it I will panic, so I focus on getting the pod away, there is so little time. There is black smoke and fire all around me as the door opens underneath the mothership and I come out. I set course for the planet that I was looking at only a few moments before."

"Can you see anyone else heading for the planet?"

"Yes, there are many. I see the ships that have the children."

Glenda reached out and screamed, "The children, their ships are being destroyed, the beautiful children."

We had to stop, as Glenda was unable go on. Her body was shivering, tears were running down her face, and she was sobbing uncontrollably. It took several minutes before she was able to continue.

Glenda grabbed my hand, and this seemed to calm her. I tried to reassure her, "It's all in the past. This is just a memory. Everything is okay now. Do you feel you can continue?"

"Yes, I'm all right now."

"Okay, are any of these children connected to you?"

"I don't have any sons and daughters, but I have family. All the children in those ships, they were so precious."

"Yes, let's move on now. You have broken away from the mother ship and are trying to save the crystals. Are you in communication with the others?"

"I am tuning into what they are saying, but I don't want to interfere with them because their consciousness is taken up with trying to move away from the ship and detect where the assault is coming from. They are all trying to put their shields up and maneuver. Some of them get away. Two ships are going off on a tangent, trying to get away from whatever is bombarding them.

"Because I am in a small pod, I weave a path through all the debris. If they think I am a part of it, they are less likely to hit me. There is another ship off to my right, but it is having a difficult time because it has been damaged. It goes down very fast into the water, but they are still all right. The ship is damaged but not destroyed. I try to stay close to this ship as my pod goes into the water. I sense that I am near the others, but I can't see them. I hope that I am close enough so that they will know I am there.

"I go down and down into the water, and I can see that it's very beautiful. A stream of light comes from the communication crystal, telling me to release the hatch of the pod and follow the light upwards. The crystal tells me to leave it there and just look after myself for the moment. I move upwards, gently moving my feet and hands."

"Now I am above the water, and there is this little brown being with beautiful eyes that are filled with love. I feel such a joy because there is a God light coming from this being. The little creature leads me to the shore.

"I seem to be very still, my lower limbs are still in the water. I don't seem to be moving at all. There is darkness and then there is light. Someone is coming. There is a group of them. They have these long robes and cloaks around them. Their leader is holding this big staff, like a sceptre. They are coming across the water in a procession, and they seemed really pleased to see me, they are joyful."

"What do you see after that?"

"I seem to be floating above the mountains somewhere. There is a vortex pulling me. I feel there is a little round hut made of branches. There is a dirt floor and a beautiful woman who is so loving and tender. She is tall with long hair. Her skin is sort of a honey colour. She holds me in her strong arms and sings to me.

"There are others around with black hair on their heads. Some of the older ones look like gorillas, and they are quite big. They all live in huts that are built in a circle with a fire in the middle. The fire is important, it must never go out."

"Are there any star people around?"

"Yes, some of the elders. They are quite tall and they shine."

Glenda's face changed and began to glow with an almost serene look, "The beautiful woman is my mother, and now she has a new baby, a little girl."

For the next hour, Glenda slept peacefully.

Since the day I met her, I have always felt close to Glenda. I never really knew why until this rainy day came. In that other life, the male being rescued the communication crystal, and gave his life trying to get it to Egarina. I wondered if Egarina knew in that distant time that the communication crystal lay beneath the waters of the Earth, just out of reach. Perhaps she did.

I walked outside to watch the sun as it hovered on the horizon in a glorious cradle of rainbow coloured clouds. Life was good again, and for a while, everything seemed to make sense.

CHAPTER 8

Frederic's Regression
Peter's Regression

family friend suggested that his son Frederic come and see me. At first, I spoke to Frederic on the phone. He said, "Throughout my life I've experienced periods in which information has been passed on to me by those whom I will call my guides. I do not know if the information is for me, or for someone around me, because it is not easy for me to understand or assimilate."

I invited him to come to Alcheringa,. When he arrived I sat him down with the Alcheringa stone and showed him photographs of the hieroglyphs at Kariong. What follows is his regression.

"I can see it quite clearly, this is what I saw before at another time. The thing that is most pronounced is the vegetation, it is very dense rain forest. I am walking along a trail. On the trail, there are circular disks. It seems that on this particular path, the disks are blue, spaced on the ground seven or eight feet apart."

"What are they for?" I asked.

"They seem to be simply path markers, because a lot of us are very disorientated by where we are. This is early on, perhaps a few weeks after arrival. Now I have stopped and I don't seem to be able to move forward. I am much taller than I am now, with spindly limbs. The bones seem to be almost visible, and my skin is somewhat translucent."

"Can you tell me what the colour of your skin is?"

"I would be tempted to say grey, but it's not grey, it's more like the colour of moonstone. I am not feeling well. There is a bacterial growth that seems to be affecting all of us. I feel tired, drained of energy. There is a pain at the base of my head that goes down through my spine."

"Have you been injured?"

"No, it's like we've been infected by something, and this is affecting our central nervous system. It is also influencing the blood circulation. Everyone is feeling tired and listless."

"Did this come from a mosquito or other insect?"

"That would seem possible, we all seemed to have succumbed to this infection very quickly. I have also been bitten by some kind of animal."

"Could this have been a snake?"

"No, not a snake or a mosquito, but a rather large animal that flies like a bat. What I sense is not familiar to me. It would be like a combination of a bat and a monkey, something like that."

"Can you see this animal now?"

"Everything I am telling you I am seeing, as in the pathway that I am on. This happened at night, and I did not see it very well.

"It's very hot. Much of our technology does not seem to function on this planet, not like it did on our home worlds. Some form of generating system has been established, but it overheats and explodes. The sun is definitely hotter."

"Are you being burned?"

"Me and the others are suffering from heat stroke."

"Where did you come from?"

"The **Pleiadean** star system."

Frederic was one of us. "How did you get here?"

"By ship, our ship is all right."

"Is this a small ship or a big ship?"

"Small."

"Where is the bigger ship?"

"I can see it, but what I am seeing is a memory of what it looked like. The ship was very big. It would seem that it is gone. There were two different forms of laser weapons, one that would simply destroy, and another that would dematerialise. The mothership seems to have been dematerialised, but there is talk that it was taken, and still intact. Because there is no wreckage, there is suspicion. I feel that it was destroyed, and what little was left went into the water. This is my conjecture, it is not any fact that I know.

"There were only a few ships that actually landed safely, maybe three. Much of our technology is in place at another location. There are many tools that make land clearing and survival very easy, but we are afraid to go there."

"What are the people like that are with you?"

"There are two different races. Of the two, one are Pleiadean based, the other is a combination of Arcturians and Siriuns."

"Are there any other of these races on the Earth?"

"Not at this stage. It seems that later there were encounters, but not in the early stages."

"Do you know why you came here?"

"I came to provide technical support and assistance. My role was never to be a permanent settler. Those who chose to settle seem to be from another race. What comes to me is *Altair*."

"Are there any survivors that you are close to?"

"Of my group of three, two have already died of illness after landing."

"Do you survive?"

"Yes, for a little while. I feel responsible for what has gone wrong. I am guilty and ashamed."

"You feel responsible?"

"Yes, there is an intense feeling of this in my body and I do not know how to release it."

"Why do you feel this way?"

"I gave information to a source that I thought would be friendly about the plans of colonisation."

A strange feeling came over me, "Did this information have something to do with the attack?"

"The attack was already planned. The information I gave them was for navigation."

I sat up, "What do you mean the attack was already planned, wasn't this supposed to be a time of peace?"

There was a very long pause.

Frederic's face began to contort as if he were having a strong emotional experience, "The information I gave was in good faith. It was not contrary to the wishes of my superiors. The information seemed to be freely transmitted. It was not my fault, but I still feel responsible. My feeling is that I made a mistake in judgment of who I gave information to. There were no strict controls on information. I feel that I was being used."

"By whom?" I demanded.

"By our own people."

The feeling of betrayal that I felt when I first went to Kariong rushed up inside of me. I recall speaking very loudly here, "Who amongst your own people, the hierarchy?"

"I had no part in that. My mind was very clear before this trip. Now there is great confusion, anger, and guilt. You see, I had never experienced betrayal before. I find it very difficult to let go of these feelings. They are a combination of righteousness at being sure that I did the right thing, yet feeling guilty for thinking that it was my own inability to discern who I should impart information to. This created an overwhelming feeling of anger at being betrayed by superiors."

I knew that feeling of anger, "Was this before or after you came to the Earth?" "Before. Something happened."

"What happened?"

"Things changed. There was an invasion of beings onto the mothership."

"By who?"

"Some race of beings that were disguised as Pleiadean. They were part of a conspiracy. They said they were trying to stop the Federation to establish good will. I see underground caverns, a green light, and people being enslaved."

"Are you with them?"

"Yes, we are underground, inside a dark black planet, and a prison. I was singled out to look after some of my people. I was able to help stop them from rebelling. I helped to impart knowledge of futility, given the present situation. I was able to gain some respect from our captors. It seems that I was offered to become a commander of my people who were there, and in return for keeping them quiet I was given teachings. This group does not support a federation. They seem to be able to move freely into different bodies. This race is not bad, it is just fearful.

"Now I remember, A bat bit me, and it was rabid. I am dying from that poison. It is quite extraordinary. That is why I can no longer move on the trail. Everything is dark in the sense of having no structure. There is a pinprick sensation, and then there is a tunnel. This is completely different. The tunnel is filled with light. I feel like I stay around there for a little bit, and then I feel the sensation of coming back."

"Wait, can you tell me more about this conspiracy?"

"I feel much shorter than I was before. I see himself as a little Orang-utan. I make the people laugh. My name is *Per-la-sing*. I am so little, like a third of the height of what I was before."

"Yes, that's it. Go back to the previous life where you are still on the mothership. You must tell me, I have to know."

Frederic was either not hearing me or not listening, "My mother died giving birth to me. I was brought up by someone who doesn't look like I do, but her face looks like I used to be. She was tall, and came from Lyra. The person who looked after me was a very good friend. That person was you."

Frederic opened his eyes. Then he looked at me with a quizzical expression, "Your face looks so strange. Did I say something wrong?"

The reading from Frederic was completely unexpected. I did not know whether to accept it or not. For a while, I put it off as being some kind of misinterpretation on my part or that of Frederic. It seemed inconceivable that something like he described could have happened, for the hierarchy to knowingly allow the people on the mother ship to be destroyed. I could see no reason.

Then came Peter. I met him at a seminar workshop in Hong Kong. Several months later he called me and asked for a meeting, saying that he was experiencing an inner conflict, and feeling that he needed to see me. I agreed, thinking that he might have something to say that would add to the star people story.

He settled into the hot seat and viewed the photographs from Kariong. He did not seem to have any particular reaction to them, but I asked him anyway, "Can you see yourself on the mothership?"

His eyes closed tightly and he sighed deeply, "Before I arrived, I travelled from a planet somewhere and transferred to the ship. I seemed to be brought to the ship in passing, as if I was meant to join it at some point. The planet I came from was green."

"Tell me what you look like."

"I am not like them. I am the only one here from the green planet. I have very white patches on my palms and the inside of my arms. The rest of my skin is dark and swarthy. I feel that my head is very small, and it extends forward from the rest of my body. There is like a kink in my neck. There are no fingernails on my hands, and no thumb. I have four fingers on each hand.

"I feel as if I am going to the ship to meet someone. I feel like I am quite important actually."

"Who is bringing you to the ship?"

"Oh, I've got this real attitude, I can tell you. These people are definitely subordinates. Well it's not really for me to say that, but it feels like these are unimportant minions in the scheme of things. They are the ones that are driving this little shuttle ship. It's a very small ship, and I am sitting in the only seat. I really feel quite important."

"Do the others in the ship look like you?"

"They are blue and white, but not all the same. One of them is pear shaped, the others look relatively human."

"How do they regard you?"

"They are a bit afraid of me, perhaps intimidated, because I do feel as if I have some kind of authority. When we arrive, they stand back as I walk through to the mothership. I should say strutting more than walking. It is very bright inside the mothership, and it takes a while for my eyes to adapt. The other ship was quite dark inside. I feel disconnected from the person that I am experiencing. He can't lighten up because he has things to do."

"Is anyone there to meet you?"

"Yes, there are three people that look like the one with the pear shaped body. I have the feeling that they are reptilian but they are not. They have skin that is like a shark, and their faces are in three layers."

"Are you troubled about anything?"

"Nope, I've got a real mission, a purpose. Everybody recognises me. They are following me and talking among themselves. I feel as if I am in a hurry because the ship is leaving. I am laughing at someone. This person runs the ship and we are laughing."

"What does he look like?"

"He looks kind of human in some ways, very pale white skin. His face is tapered towards the bottom and he is quite tall. His eyes are almond shaped, but horizontal. The head is wide at the top. He's really a jovial character, definitely a man of position, but he is laughing with me.

"The control room is kind of like Starship Enterprise, there is so much light. There are technical things around, but it all appears very simple. There are large panels of light that deliver information to the people watching them."

"Move on in time and tell me what is happening," I suggested.

"Now I feel as if I am waking up, and that I've been in a capsule or tube of some sort. My skin colour is different. It's not as brown as it was before. It's bluish like the others, although a bit darker. It seems as if I have been through some kind of transformation, I definitely feel as if I have shed something."

"Now that you are out of the capsule, do you have a role to play?"

"Hmm, I feel like I've got nothing to do at the moment. I am just waiting to arrive at where the ship is heading. I am watching what seems like a computer-generated display of the solar system at the moment. This is on one of those large screens. There are different names for the planets. The first planet is Zun, Varn is the second, Mu is the third, Zaron is the fourth, and there is one called June. The orbits are all drawn in. There are more planets shown here than in today's solar system.

"I feel a bit of trepidation or excitement, an 'at last' feeling, or something that I have worked towards. I have coordinates that they need to feed into their system, something to do with getting where we are going. I've got information about the location."

"Oh, are you some sort of navigator?" I asked.

"I don't know where I fit in, it's like I have a key of some sort. Something is dependent on the information that I put into their machine. It is the time and place that this whole thing comes together. This is actually done by hand, because I just put my hand on this machine and the diagram changes. All the planets have moved except the Mu planet, which is now static. I feel as if this is information that is needed at the last minute. Each time I touch it, the planets change position, and we get closer. When we arrive, the ship cannot go through the cloud layer. Now it's standing still and just drifting with the planet. Smaller ships are required to travel to the surface. There is someone on the planet that I must contact."

"Why is that?"

"I am a go between, a diplomat. I have contacts with this planet that these other people don't have. That's why I have the coordinates."

"Does this have something to do with peace?"

"Yes, definitely. I feel as if we are going to meet somebody, and the commander is coming too. The scout ship lands on a flat surface, like a pyramid with the top cut off."

"The reptilians that meet us are quite ornate, and they wear a lot of gold. They are a red-brown people, and they act self- important, I feel quite nervous about it. There is a negotiation or something.

"There is going to be a hand-over, a passing of the baton, and these people dressed in ornate clothing are going to leave with great pomp and splendour. They want to keep face."

"Are they happy about that?"

"Yeah. There are these other people as well, like minions or something. These are lesser beings, but they look quite human actually. Their heads are narrow, with big ears. They have five fingers that are long. They seem like slaves.

"The scout ship departs with the others, leaving me behind. One of the ornate ones looks at me and asks, 'Is now the time?' I say, 'Yes, it is.' Then I give them instructions to carry on about their business.

"It's night time, and I am checking off items on a list as larger ships arrive with blue people. They offload supplies and machinery. Some are assembling a kind of beacon device, others are unloading conical shaped cylinders that contain seeds and spores.

"Again there is a feeling of trepidation and mistrust. Now I am watching the mothership evacuate because it is under attack. Many little ships are leaving towards the planet. There is an energy stream going into the ship and exploding inside it. I feel quite calm as I stand with the commander, as if it were expected."

It was happening again, "Did you say it was expected?"

"Yes I feel like it was, it certainly was not unexpected."

"What about the commander, did he expect it too? I mean, what is he doing and saying?"

"He is just giving orders and the two of us are watching, both quite disconnected, not panicking."

There was a long pause. A funny kind of feeling came over me. I began to prompt him, "The commander, he went down with the ship didn't he?"

"I don't know, I'm out of there. I've gone in another ship, and he didn't come with me. We are heading to the planet really fast. There are definitely some ships that don't make it. The one I am in hits the water."

I sat up straight, "Yes, that's right, one hits the water. You say you're in the ship that hits the water."

"Yeah. There is a major sort of pull as it hits. I am getting a cross section of where it has landed in the water. It's like a lake."

"A lake? Could it have possibly been in Broken Bay?"

"It could be any place, but it definitely feels like a lake. I can't identify exact places for some reason, but I know what's going on. Now it's going through the water, down under a lip and up the other side into a cavernous kind of place. These ships are amphibious."

At that moment, I thought of the sea caves that are on the headlands, not too far from Broken Bay. Maybe another one of the landing craft from the mother ship had landed there and taken refuge in the caves. This could be a new discovery, but why was I hearing of it for the first time after so many regressions? Perhaps they were unable to get out, "Do you feel that your ship is trapped in there?"

"Trapped in the sense that if it goes out it's in trouble. But it's inside the land. There is all this activity, and there are other ships in there as well. I thought the ship was crashing, but it's not. There are quite a number of ships in this huge cavern, and there are lots of little people running around."

Hmm, the caverns I was thinking about aren't that big, and he was talking about many ships. This was getting confusing.

"Are there any lizard like people in the cavern?"

"No, none."

"Are there any people off the ship with you?"

"Yeah, lot's. There is definitely a lot of stuff going on here, the little slave-like creatures are off-loading things, like salvaging what they can, that kind of thing. There is machinery as well, very metallic and silver. There is a lot of heat on at the moment, and everyone is in a hurry. There is a feeling of 'it's done' or something is done, and it's irreversible."

"Did you know 'it' was going to happen?"

"I feel like I did know actually. I didn't feel that it was unexpected. All these people are panicking, yet they knew where this place was, and they knew we could get into this cavern through the water. It's inside the land, I mean it, and it's not just a cave, it's a really huge cavern. You have to go through water to get into it, and it's all lit up."

"So, what do the other people look like that are on board the ship?"

"Some are of the pear shaped variety I spoke of, but most of them are slim people with a shark kind of skin."

"Do you have some sort of connection with the lizard people to know these others?"

"Some kind of connection? Yeah, I was the go between."

"Do you know of any survivors from the mothership?"

"If they survived, I have no idea where they could have gone."

Something was wrong here, nothing would gel, "Well, move on a bit and tell me what happens then."

"This is quite a long time later, years maybe. Everything is now settled, and much of the community is still under the land. But almost all of the equipment and stuff I saw earlier has been brought outside. There is definitely seeding going on outside. The slaves are doing it."

"Can you look at your body again and tell me what it looks like?"

"Now it's brown again. That's weird. I've reverted back to the way I was before I entered the mothership. I think I've adapted to the environment. They are leaving by the way, the ships that have survived are actually leaving, because this thing has been established against all odds."

"Where are they going?"

"Back home. The little ships are making an effort to go back home. It's like they're all heading out. Because there is no mothership, they're going to try to make it on their own. I don't hold out any hope, and I'm not going with them."

"Do you know what happens to them?"

"No, they just disappear. They waited and waited until it was safe. The lizard people think the whole thing has been destroyed, and the other people have gone. There was definitely a new civilisation being developed, with all this food and technology that helped start it off."

"Was this still inside the Earth?"

"No, they had started transporting this stuff outside to grow things. They used the seeds and spores that were inside the cones they had taken and stored. There is a time lapse here you know, I feel I've gone on for a long time. What had happened was a new civilisation was starting, based on the deposits that were left from the mother ship."

Nothing was fitting anymore, "Okay, for the moment, go back to the mothership with all the people on board, when the lizard like people went back on their word and attacked the ship."

"Yes, the problem is that not all of the equipment or materials were able to be transported. It was like starting off with only half the materials."

"Uh yes, can you look around and see if the commander-in-chief is there?"

"Actually, there is someone else there as well. As I look around I see someone else, a similar type of being."

"Like a brother?"

"Yes."

I thought hard for a moment, "Ah yes, the commander's brother got away in an escaping ship, but that crashed into the sea. He died on that ship."

Peter nodded his head, "I saw that one, and it definitely crashed big time. You know, it did not look as if anybody could have survived."

At least one thing had become clear. Peter was not on the ship that went into the water. I wanted to reassure him, "But they did, there were people on board that survived."

Peter smiled, "Good."

Perhaps Peter had been killed and was viewing this in the after life, "Do you feel you were still around at that time, or did you come in later?"

"Still around."

"You have to be very careful at what you are looking at, you are tending to run it all together, and I am trying to separate it. Can you actually see yourself surviving from the mothership after you knew that the lizard people had gone back on their word? You must have felt very badly about that."

"A little bit."

"Only a little bit?"

"Well you see it wasn't really unexpected. I really felt that before it happened there would be time to off-load every-thing. Unfortunately there wasn't, they were too quick in their turnaround."

"Yes, but that hadn't been discussed with the commander had it, that they could go against their word?"

"No, and I was trying to negotiate things so they wouldn't. I was trying to make it as easy as possible for them to get things out. That was the point of the negotiations. I feel like some kind of intergalactic diplomat, you know. It was really important that it happened, it was just a matter of buying time."

"Why do you say that it was really important that it happened?"

"Because of all this stuff that they were bringing on this mothership. It was extremely important that it found its way into this new civilisation. Everyone knew that they would need it to re-establish a civilisation that was somewhere else on the planet."

That rather seemed to fit, "Yes, it was like a new garden. Actually, it had been planned long before the lizard like people had taken over the Earth, and then they had been expelled. You must have had a role in helping them do that. Can you go back to the mother ship at the time when it exploded? Did you actually die along with the commander-in-chief?"

"No."

"Just think about that carefully, you know it's actually possible that when you die you do not realise it at that moment. I want you to have a look and see if you really did leave your body at that point and then perhaps come into another body."

Peter appeared to think hard about it, "Well, that part in between, there is a break because I do not know how I got from the ship into the cave."

I nodded, "I think you will find that you actually did leave the body, that your body was destroyed along with the ship."

"But there seems to be such continuity of leadership in my mind."

"Yes, I think you do draw from past experiences and abilities, and these are used in the next life. Perhaps it was a long time afterward that you went into the cave under the Earth. Well, I think we've almost finished here, is there anything else you would like to look at?"

"Well there is definitely this guilt thing."

"You have a guilt thing?"

"Yes, the word guilt just comes straight into me."

"Is that because you, as a diplomat, found that all along it was not working?"

"Well, I was trying to make it work, but I just couldn't talk my way around it."

I threw my shoulders back, "Yes, and you were actually misleading the commander as well, because you were saying one thing to him while knowing that the reptiles weren't going to agree. Is your guilt because you knew that you were just putting up a show?"

"But his commanders also knew."

My jaw dropped, "Did you say his commanders knew?"

Peter nodded, "That's why they called me, that's why I was brought in. The people that sent him as commander, they all knew. He had no knowledge of what he was getting into, and I couldn't tell him because the hierarchy brought me in. They wouldn't tell anybody, otherwise there would have been a big fear thing, and they didn't want it that way."

My face flushed and I felt faint. I needed something I could find comfort in, "Okay Peter, one last time, go back to ship just before the attack. Look at the commander, tell me what he does, tell me what he says."

Peter's face looked thoughtful, "Well, he turned to the particle beam operator and said 'Shoot, shoot."

Symbol on rocks at Kariong

Symbols on rocks at Kario

CHAPTER 9

Tom's Regression
Steven's Regression
Alcheringa Explains the Conspiracy

I walked away from that regression with a feeling of dismay. The implication seemed quite clear, it was known beforehand by the organisers of the mission to Earth that the star people would be destroyed. For several days, I walked around trying to rationalise the situation. Some of those I had regressed expressed the feeling that what they were experiencing was just imagination. For a while, I wanted to rationalise Peter's reading as just that. Then along came Tom.

Tom smiled as he viewed the photographs of Kariong, "Yes, I am near the ship. The experience is being channelled through. I seem to have an air of authority about me."

"Are you getting the feeling of being on the ship?"

"Not yet, but I am feeling different. My emotions are very clear, but all this appears to be my imagination."

"Let that go. Look down and tell me what your body looks like."

As Tom looked down, his eyes closed, and he waved his arms gently about, "I sense the body is very slight in build, but not frail. The arms are thin. The torso is fairly slender. It is quite healthy and strong. There is no hint of malnourishment or sickness, even though the body is so thin. There is some kind of organ between the legs that looks tubular like. It seems to be a very simple appendage that retracts into the body.

"I'm getting a glimpse of a place where there is a lot of light, perhaps it's the ship. The control consoles are very streamlined and there are no knobs or switches. In the middle of the room there is a bridge, perhaps this is more to the front.

"Yes of course, it is mind power, the vibration of thought that creates the propulsion of this ship as it navigates through multi- dimensional realms. There is a telepathic guidance system. This is an advanced technology."

"How does this guidance system operate?"

"By a person receiving or transmitting data or information. This particular device is amplifying brain waves to go to a designated place. There are crystalline structures that focus these energies."

"Are there any others around you at the moment?"

"Yes, there are others. I can see silhouettes, long slender shapes standing around the bridge at their workstations, doing what they have to do. I am getting a feeling that beneath the bridge there are very many people. This is a special mission. I am feeling honoured that I can be in it."

I wanted to find out what ship we were in immediately, "Yes, can you see the Commander around?"

"He is telling me something. There is a question about the ship's duties. I am to maintain the daily running of the ship, and to counsel and advise him in the decision making process. The commander seems a bit anxious."

"Do you know what he is anxious about?"

"He is kind of keeping it quiet. I think he suspects something may be up."

"Is this before the mission started, or on the journey?"

"On the journey itself."

"Move forward in your memory to where the ship arrives at Earth."

"We have landed in a bush-type setting, and I can see that we are in this new and unpleasant environment. It seems there are some who are wounded. I am outside the ship where we have set up a sort of camp, because we have to stay. There are people who appear to be affected by the elements of this place. Some consideration is being given to sustenance. This wasn't a problem while we were travelling on the ship, but in this place, it is definitely something that we need to think about. I can see a group of people that need help. There is a lot of sadness and disappointment, isolation, and emotional pain."

"Are you feeling that way as well?"

"I sense an overwhelming fear and suffering also, but I have to maintain control of my situation. You see I have a duty as second in command to look after the welfare of the others. I must maintain and put my fears aside. I must start to organise the people in groups so that we can function adequately in this place."

"Do you feel responsible in some way for all these people being injured?"

"No, I was doing my duty. I did it to the best of my ability. There were times in the aftermath when I could have handled things better, but nevertheless we all did our best with what resources we had."

"Move back to the mothership, just before you landed on Earth."

"It appears that we have an incursion with other ships. We seem to be under attack. It's like an ambush, and we have taken heavy losses."

"How do you feel about that?"

"A bit surprised, we didn't expect it."

"What did you expect?"

"We expected this to be easy. We have a glorious mission to perform for the sake of the galaxy. There is a feeling of jubilation and happiness because of what we are going to be involved in. It's a rescue mission. We are going to help free beings from the bondage of slavery and darkness. We have the sanction of God and the council who sent us."

"Can you tell me more about the Council that sent you?"

"It is made up of representatives of different worlds."

"Do you have any idea of the different worlds, which races?"

"There are representatives from almost all the worlds, including those that are not of the light, so that every species, every world, has a say."

"There are those that are more important than others, meaning some posts of responsibility and control on the council are held by certain species. But everyone is involved. They can express their opinion and vote through the council. They are in agreement about most things, especially when it comes from the light. The council is aligned with the light."

"How does the council act on this mission, the one to Earth?"

"They sacrifice us."

That statement kind of jolted me, "Why would they sacrifice you?"

"Because of failed negotiations with certain other species. There was also a bigger picture in play, although none of us could see it at the time."

"Could you put that into words now?"

"The crashed species needed to stay and create a civilisation. The repercussions of this would create the initial goal of bringing light to this place, and freeing it from the bondage of slavery and darkness. That is the bigger picture. This is the way the events unfolded.

"There was a theme, that of the sacrificial lamb, a sacrifice where these people took a heavy loss at the hands of other races. Because of that, the planet was able to move on. The rebuilding process, the overcoming of obstacles, created the desired effect.

"It wasn't conquest over the enemy that won the fight, it was conquest over adversity, fear of turmoil and darkness that brought light to this place. These people were able to create something new and worthwhile in this place, but that was all but forgotten. Everyone thought they had lost, but in fact, it was through staying and persevering that they won. My task is done."

Thinking he was saying that this was the end of his regression, I reached over to turn off the tape recorder, and then paused, "Do you have anything else you would like to say?"

"Yes, there was a third in Command who was a Judas, who betrayed the ship to save himself from pain and hardship. He secretly negotiated a deal with the Draco, and through this deal, he put the others in peril while trying to save himself. I don't know what happened to this person, but there is more to say about this matter."

I sat upright and looked at him. I wasn't sure that I wanted to hear this.

Tom continued, "He had a poor character trait. There was a weakness there. I tell you solemnly the deal was very simple one.

"It was about saving his life amongst the chaos and barbarity that went on. The third in command had an inkling of what was going to happen because of his conspiracy with the Draco. He was aware of the reneging and that a trap had been set. His main condition was that he escaped from the turmoil with his life intact and his loved ones too.

"He knew what the galactic council was trying to do. He also knew of the enemy, and the Draco plan not to follow their promise. He knew both sides of the coin, and was thus in a position of knowing how the voyage would end. The third in command of the Rexegena wanted to escape from the attack with his life.

"His is a very simple story, basically one of greed and self interest on his part. Obviously there was something in it for him. There were big rewards from the Draco side for his cooperation. Yet, he was playing it two ways. He had both sides of the coin. He had privilege and authority on the galactic council side, and was given rewards of a monetary kind from the Draco on the other. He was in a position to know what was going to happen, and he was in a position to bargain with the Draco. This person was from the Pleiadean people. He was one of the ones respected by the council, with high standing in society.

"He had a distinguished record and career. He had moved up through the ranks with honour, with merit, and was well respected. But he fell foul to temptation at the end and was bribed. It was just for wealth that they tempted him. He had a weakness in the area of material possessions.

"It was no coincidence he was planted amongst the crew of this ill-fated voyage. This was all part of the heavenly plan. You could say that he was the one who put his signature on this plan when he dropped the shields of the Rexegena just before the attack."

At that point, I ended the session myself. The anger and sense of betrayal that I felt overshadowed my desire to hear any more.

I spent several days thinking about Tom's regression. Was that why the *Binjala* personality in Steven's regression laughed when he talked about the mission? What was it he said? 'We gave them assurances that it would be organised and safe. That is what we told them.' I wanted to know, so I called Steven and asked him to come and see me.

After almost marching Steven to the hot seat, he connected immediately and identified himself as *Binjala* from the **Elohim**. For a moment, I had the funny feeling this was all being arranged. I asked him to explain why he laughed when we were talking about fifty thousand star people not succeeding on their mission to the planet Earth.

Steven looked at me with the smallest of smiles, "The soul body of the star people was the sense of what was being moved from planet to planet. With the extra violence during the transfer of physical bodies from one location to another, the manifestation of their consciousness became very different. There has to be a time when you abandon the body, you can do that whenever you like. We initially suggested to the council that the star people leave their bodies earlier on, before any sort of travel. Hence, they would travel interstellar space without a body.

"That was the plan we had set down. They decided instead that the star people would abandon their bodies on Earth in order to leave resonance of their physical form. As I said before, they thought it would hold a value to their sense of community, and all the rest of it."

"What about the laugh?" I demanded.

"The laugh was in regards to this beautiful change to the plan, for it was indeed a divine addition. Now we would not only take their soul bodies, but the resonance of their physicality as well. We thought this was a wonderful idea."

How could something this horrific make sense? "This was supposed to be of more benefit to the plan, is that what you are saying?"

"Yes indeed, much more benefit. For then we, as individuals incarnating onto the Earth, could explore both the psychic and physical remnants of the culture left by the star people. This is very stimulating to us in our physical manifestations on this Earth."

"So you weren't actually laughing at them?"

"No, not at all, we were laughing with them, with their souls. Their decision was made at the soul level. It was very beautiful indeed. It was marvellous. The laugh had nothing to do with their physical destruction. I mean the destruction of a physical form is a painful experience, but it's just physical pain."

It was all still confusing to me, "Then why did you express yourself with a laugh?"

"Well, in a conversation with words on any level, a laugh is simply a representation of a build up or excitement of energy.

We were talking about the star people's physical movement from one place to the other, as well as a description of their choice to give up their bodies, which as I said, was a soul choice. The conversation required some response, and I gave a positive response. Do you understand?"

I shook my head, "I'm not sure that I do, nor can I understand the response itself. A laugh would suggest that you were laughing at them, or that you doubted their ability to understand what they were doing."

Steven smiled and waved his hand, "You need to understand that although it caused more physical suffering and a greater awareness of the extreme attachment to the physical form, it was for a much higher good. They themselves as souls were perfectly aware of it. So, I was congratulating their soul choice. It was a very brave decision to make, particularly given the circumstances of their physical trauma. But even that has proven to be helpful to us. Now we can relax a bit more when the time comes for our physical bodies to be left, for we know that we will be involved in continuing incarnations on a single planet, in a body that is designed to reach for the light."

An eerie feeling came over me, "You make it sound as if all this was done for Reptoids, Dinoids, and Draco."

"Well, yes."

Then I had the unnerving realisation that all I had to do to find out exactly what had happened to the mission, from the other side, was to ask. So, I did, "From your viewpoint, tell me what happened after the mothership arrived."

Steven's face broke into a wide grin, as if he had been waiting for me to ask, "I had taken on a lizard form in order to influence the lizard king and his queen. It was very easy for me to take on a physical form. I was acting as an advisor.

Whenever they were in a quandary about what was happening with the approaching star ship, I would offer advice.

"I had in mind a grand plan to integrate the different species of the Earth with the star people, but knew the lizards would never take to that directly. I just steered them unwittingly in the right direction. In order for the lizards to take my advice, it had to be clear to them they would be the ones who would benefit, and so my options were very limited. But, successful integration was the highest aim. My voice in the ear of the lizard king became more complex towards the end as the ship was approaching.

"We had double agents out in the field, and these occasional 'diplomats' would make a trip up to the ship to discuss some of the details for the safe and auspicious arrival of the star people. That was the cover story. It was what we told their officials, those who seemed secure in their beliefs.

"The other part of the plan, of course, was to find weak links in the higher echelons of the star people's command, to try and cut deals with them. We were interested in their technology more than anything else. A few of their tools, a few of their pieces of machinery would be invaluable to us in our wars against the Cat people, controlling the Dinoids, as well as developing newer and more capable species of ape-like creatures to do our gold mining.

"So, we sounded them out. We would find a person, hold a meeting, a little one on one, or one on two discussions with the star people, and offer them a deal. At first it came across quite well, all were interested in where we were coming from, saying things to us like, 'Could you spare us a little laser?' We would always say, 'Oh of course, take this one as a gift of our show of friendship.' As time went on, and more and more exchanges were made, larger deals were being asked for, and more machinery given, 'Where are you dropping your equipment around the planet?' we would ask. After all, they had been making drops here and there on the planet."

"Thus we knew that they had other landing sites, other places where some of their technology was resting, where some of the genetic experiments would be carried out that nobody else knew about. Now we could come down, have a look in detail, and learn something. If, under some circumstance, communication with the mothership was disabled, or destroyed, or simply not available, we could acquire the entire lot for ourselves.

"So there I was, asking for this sort of information, in exchange for perhaps some sweetening of your personal landing deal, hah hah, and so on.

"Some of the deals we were making became riskier for the star person involved. It would involve compromising their position, compromising their respect for their own authority. But the deals we were making were even sweeter. We did have something to offer of course. Even the idea of some of the white gold powder, for a start, seemed quite attractive. We wouldn't spare any of course, but we would always simply offer. And, I shouldn't forget, the arrangements were made for the big day the ship was to land for the ceremony.

"As Binjala, I had been making occasional visits to the ship myself, not always in guise. I would sometimes appear as a diplomat, but I would not necessarily let the lizards know that I had left on their behalf, not always. This way I could learn more for certain, and not have to report back.

"I had been making some sweeter deals, even finding out the locations of their previous genetic experiments on their home planets and, even better than that, accessing the information gained from the experimental results. Now this was, of course, purely confidential information amongst the star people, but I had found out, they had been compromised.

"The deals were becoming quite complicated. I was beginning to suspect, and had told the king so, that some of our recruits on the mothership had considered telling their own people about what they were up to, which was extremely dangerous to the total smoothness of transition we were trying to express.

"There was of course the golden opportunity, the actual time of the hand-over. Alcheringa and Egarina were going to be on the ground. The lizard king and his queen would be in presence. So, I could make a trip up in my Binjala guise, officially and unofficially, and talk to some of the people high up amongst the ranks, without the possible interference of their commander. This was a perfect opportunity to go and have a chat, to see what I could arrange.

"Alcheringa's energy is totally absorbed in making this run smoothly, protecting himself physically because he does have suspicions that this isn't going to go as cool as it is supposed to. Still, they all have to continue, and to complicate matters they are not completely sure what is going on. I had been fortunate enough to not let that information pass on. So I take a trip up, just myself.

"One of the lesser recruits that I had been speaking to, about making this sweeter deal in exchange for the results of the genetic experiments, had told one of his superiors. There I was, in a very difficult position.

"I knew the chips were going to be down, so I tried to offer this superior a deal that if he could give me the particulars of the experiments, it would be very useful.

"That didn't work so I told him, 'We are going to destroy you. This is your only chance you realise? You can give me the information now, or we can just blow you up anyway. So, if you want to have a chance of your species survival, you can just tell me straight away. This is a rare opportunity. You see your whole mission, I am telling you, is going to fail. But if you give me the information, we will have some ability to perpetuate your species, in hybridised form, under the direction and supervision of the lizards.'

"He didn't like that at all, of course not. But I had to make the offer. So, I left and soon returned to talk with him along with a lizard person. I also brought a facility for the star person to read the future of this lizard persons *Akashic record*, the lizard person that would be responsible for the star peoples' destruction.

"So I sat the lizard person down, quite anaesthetised. He didn't really know what was happening, but I didn't care. I said, 'Look, play the record of what is going to happen to this lizard person and you will see that you are all going to die tomorrow.' Of course they did, and were totally in a state of shock. They knew that I was somewhat responsible for this whole thing. I told them the king and queen didn't know that I was here, although I was partly acting on their behalf, and I explained my position as being separate from the lizards. They did not seem to grab hold of this as well as I thought they could.

"So, I demonstrated an example of the technology that was going to be used to destroy them, just a small one, although it made quite a hole in one of their bigger pieces of equipment. I said to the supervisor, 'This is just a little gun, you know? We've got a cannon forty times bigger than this that is ready for you.

"Somewhat to my surprise he pointed at the lizard person and said, 'This little friend of yours will go back. He will pass on the message that we have refused your offer." Then he asked to see the little weapon that I had demonstrated, and when I gave it to him, he shot me with it. That was it.

"I'm feeling like 'Damn, I've lost the body.' Well, none of the other lizards know about it. These star people can dump my body out in space if they want, I don't care what they do. Then I decide to head back, take on another body just like the last one, for this is no problem, and turn up as usual in the king's chamber after the meeting.

"Oh, one other thing I did after I was killed was to make up a new plan to make sure this was going to work, because I had lost my voice on the Rexegena.

"There was a young boy on the ship, a volunteer from the Elohim, we were quite good friends already. I said to him, 'If you would come on down, you can get out of this if you like. You have one choice, you are going to die tomorrow.' He said, 'Yes, I believe you.' I said, 'What you need to do is get yourself into the body of this particular little upstanding ape-like creature, down on the ground in the morning. I can help you do that.' He says, I am willing to do that.

"Now he has a lot more talent than most of them. My little friend does the part I ask him to. He enters the little ape like creature and I put some of myself in there too, and the bait is set. Now this little ape-like creature is having a very weird time of it and starts acting strange. So, he is picked up by the lizard guards and taken to be fed to the Draco.

The lizards offer the 'sacrifice' of this little slave in return for the apparition of the Draco/emperor, who will give them instructions on what to do, now that this little farce of a changeover ceremony is over. But instead of the Draco/ emperor apparition, what they get is an apparition produced by me. I make the new Draco/emperor say, 'Blow up the ship.' He says it, the lizards dutifully obey, and it is done. The soul of the little boy moved into free space, relieved of the trauma of the destruction. That was our agreement."

"The star people thought they could stop this from happening by destroying me, because I was the emissary of that information. But I made it happen anyway. Do you have any questions?"

All this was difficult for me to accept, "Why would a star person be responsive to you, other than the threat of death?"

Steven laughed, "There had been somewhat of an understanding amongst themselves as the journey went on, through whispers in their ear so to speak, that there were going to be problems. They knew that there might be some element of difficulty and betrayal amongst them, which sparked just the tiniest grain of self-interest.

"As the time got closer, and they began to suspect even more that this was not going to work in a big way, offers of self-preservation became more and more appealing. We could theoretically offer them a place in our culture, although they didn't like that idea particularly. I didn't have that much more to offer, just enough to generate a small amount of insecurity. All I had to do was exchange energy with the lizards, and more insecurity would follow.

"Perhaps it was the offer of some of our technology, phrased in such a way that it would be beneficial for them and their families.

"We did not have the facilities to care for the genetic rendering of fifty thousand people, but perhaps ten or twenty we could accommodate. I would say, 'Would you like to be among these chosen few, if positions are going to be offered in that regard?' The temptation was set. We didn't have to follow it up. We just had to get the edge."

Steven paused and began staring at me like he did the first time I regressed him. I really didn't like that look at all, although the everyday Steven is a very nice sincere person. The question popped up in my mind, "Did you ever contact the survivors?"

Steven smiled again, "Well, if I may digress for a minute. It was very important, while acting for the lizards, that I maintained their strict line of thought. I could not deviate from this line too dramatically and retain an identity with them. However, I did approach the star people survivors, the first time in my indigenous form, a tall upstanding ape-like creature carrying a spear. I also did this in a variety of other forms trying to find somebody who might have more information.

"This was very difficult to do because of their distress and their social alignment. They seemed more interested in finding ways to help their fellow star people than to pass on obviously sensitive information to a foreign creature. And thus I found it difficult to acquire technology for the lizards.

"As I had influence among a few of the survivors, I took on other forms and gave very specific instructions to them on some of the beginning genetic cross types, aided them very specifically, told them which plants to use, how to prepare certain medicines, and where to find certain animals that would be suitable to engage in such activity.

"They could have done it on their own, but this made things very speedy, and it left nothing to chance. There was also the possibility that the lizard people would manage to regain some sort of societal backbone, and then come down and hunt them out. Thus, time was of the essence.

"The destruction was actually quite disturbing in a way for the lizard people. This is because it was such a major event, with so much death. Huge military activity had been aimed at someone that was clearly not an aggressor. The everyday lizard was beginning to ask 'why?' Political remedies were badly needed, so I was asked for guidance by the king. Amongst the political advice, I tried to put forth the proposition that perhaps it would be wise to be kind to some of those remaining star people, of course if only to find out other information that might be of value.

"One of the ambassadors made some pronouncement that I might perhaps be more interested in the promotion of the star people than our own. I argued that a melding was beneficial for both of us, particularly for the lizards.

"The simple notion of that intent was taken as a great act of betrayal, and my body was killed, ending my close association with the lizards. So, you might say that I died for your people."

I sent Steven away to ponder the situation.

A huge sense of anger and betrayal cut across all my feelings. Had the star people really been so naive as to allow themselves to be led down a path of lies and deception? I did not want to believe that it could be true.

Peter talked about a council that sacrificed the star people. Steven had mentioned talking to a council to suggest that the star people leave their bodies before travelling to Earth. Should I believe Peter and Steven, and if so what was this council? If it were true, why hadn't Alcheringa told me? I needed to find out, so I went to my study, sat with the Alcheringa stone, and called his name.

"It is I Alcheringa. What is troubling you my child?"

I stammered out, "Some of the people I regressed indicated a conspiracy in the mission of the Rexegena. They spoke of a council. Was there some kind of council involved in the mission?"

"Yes there was a galactic council, somewhat like your United Nations. It consisted of races from many parts of the galaxy."

"Was the decision to send the Rexegena on its mission made by this council?"

"That was a decision the council made, yes. But after the ship Rexegena set upon her journey, the conditions of what was to take place became different. There had been an agreement, one the council believed and accepted when the ship set off on its journey. However, it was found that the Reptoids went back on their word, and had no intention of leaving the planet."

"Was the council aware that the Rexegena would be destroyed?"

"No, they did not know, well, not all. As I said there were some that had agreed and went back on their word."

"Was there some kind of subterfuge at the council?"

"Indeed so. But it was not so much the members of the council as those that were involved and interacted with the council that the subterfuge existed. The council was not aware of it until later, when the realisation came upon them that indeed there was serious subterfuge."

My eyes went blink, "How could a council that is supposed to be 'Galactic' miss something like this, weren't they telepathic?"

"Yes, but like humans, they too were physical, and of a point of frequency that operates with some limit, and so mistakes were made, as often happens in many councils. Your United Nations makes errors in judgment. Surely you can see this."

"I'm not so sure that I can."

"A diplomatic mission that had been sent to interact with the Reptoids returned with glowing reports saying that the Reptoids were very willing to leave. This was, in truth, because the council had formed an edict that they should, for they had taken over this planet against the will of God. However, adjustments had to be made when they did not leave."

"What adjustments?"

"The adjustment to the knowingness the mission was doomed. There was much sadness of course. But then they sought guidance from the Elohim, and were advised from that point."

"What about Steven saying the star people were to give up their physicality in order to leave their being of light and physical imprint upon the Earth. Is that correct?"

"Yes, their decision to do this came from the guidance of the Elohim. This was done at a level that is of a different frequency. The soul operates at that frequency, and it was from that point that a new agreement was made. This happened when the realisation came that, in the physical sense, the mission was not to be successful."

I did not like what I was hearing, "Was any effort made to get these people out, or was there some alternate plan that could perhaps save their lives?"

"Once the ship Rexegena had been launched and was on her track, there was no way that she could turn back. Decisions were made at the galactic council to try to bring assistance to any of those that survived. Other than that, as I have already said, the souls had already agreed to give up their physicality upon arrival."

"When did they make this agreement?"

"After it was recognised that the plan was not going to succeed, and their souls were influenced by the Elohim. Understand that this is a different consciousness within these galactic races as it is in the earthly human. It was not the consciousness of physicality, hardly my dear, for they would not so readily have given up their lives."

It all sounded like an unconscious suicide mission to me, "Before they left, none of the star people had any conscious awareness whatsoever of what was about to happen?"

"They did not, and as I have told you, the council did not either. It was only after the ship was on its journey the realisation came there had been subterfuge, and that words were said that were not meant. These individuals were very cunning, they had completely deceived the council.

"Every effort was given to assist those that survived. Those who died came back into their light bodies to realise they had agreed to do it. It was not set in black and white the mission was going to fail, far from that. It is like any mission where adjustments have to be made when it is quite obvious one is not going to win the war. They have to draw back and rethink. That is what took place."

"Do you mean there was a war?" I asked.

"This was not a war with weapons from the star peoples' point of view, it was a war against darkness, and they were bringing the crystal light. Now they have returned to bring the story out in remembrance, and they have not lost anything. They have achieved what they set out to do. It is true the survivors experienced suffering and missed those who moved on. But now they have joined together again.

"If you look at life as eternity with no end, you will realise there is no need to worry about whether they should or should not have died in the physical, for they moved on and took on other physical bodies, they continue to incarnate back and forth. These people are the ones who have held the light throughout the ages to assist humans to evolve. It takes courage, and they have done well."

Perhaps, but the whole thing had a Draco tinge to it, "Steven said the Draco were aware of this and were pleased at the outcome before it happened."

"The Draco are of a different frequency than the council. They too are connecting to the Elohim and that frequency, for they are of the fallen angels. They had an understanding and a foreseeing of how the light source could be of benefit to them, and also knew that it would bring light to this corner of the galaxy. The Draco influenced the Reptoids to withdraw their acceptance of leaving Earth. The events that took place were pre-planned by the Draco. When they put it to the Elohim, the Elohim realised there was no way of turning back, and so they influenced the galactic council."

"To adopt the decision to let it happen?" I said.

"The Rexegena was already on its journey when the Elohim realised what the Draco really wanted all the time. Do you understand?"

"I understand what you say, going along with it is quite another matter."

"I would like you to accept that it has worked out. See it as a very positive thing. If you look at the bigger picture you will see that light has come into this corner of the galaxy, and there are many that are gaining from its coming. The reptilian form, the Draco form, and other races in this corner of the galaxy are gaining from experiencing love and compassion for the first time ever. This energy is assisting all these races to raise their frequency.

"The Elohim came to realise there was no way of helping this corner of the galaxy without working with the Draco to some degree. The galactic council's final acceptance of this was based on a request made by the Elohim.

"As time moves on, the frequency is changing and lifting all these races. Remember, God the source is the creator of all. God is pure love and compassion. This is what is infiltrating into these races as they experience the human form. The human being that was created by the star people is imbued with the crystal, or Christ energy. It is the human being that provides a level playing field for those who do not know love. Because of them, the energy of this place is now one of love."

"Why are you just telling me about this now, why not before?"

"I have been releasing information in manageable bits and pieces so that you will understand and see the bigger picture. I am very pleased that you have responded in the way you have. Thank you my child. God bless you and thank you."

CHAPTER 10

The Message from Helen Boyd
Alcheringa talks to Gerry and Margaret tells
of the legend of the Eighth White Sister
Return of the Alcheringa Stone
Egarina talks to the Eighth White Sister

The Fax machine in my study buzzed as a handwritten message emerged from its interior.

Dear Valerie,

I'm afraid it is time for the Alcheringa stone to go home. All is in place, or will be once I know it can be in Sydney by the tenth. I feel I am well enough now to get the stone back to its rightful owners. Apologies for such short notice, but this often seems to be the way of things.

179

Thank you for watching over the stone for the past two years, and for being someone I could depend on. Sorry I haven't been able to call, no energy, short of money, and ill.

I hope to be at Uluru and the McDonnell Ranges on the twenty-first. On that evening, the stone will be handed over. Please phone me to confirm.

Love and Blessings, Helen Boyd.

Later that day I rang Helen at Byron Bay, where she was staying, and offered to bring the stone to her there, as I would be passing nearby on a book tour.

It was just a matter of time, I knew that, and now the time had come. But the stone was like a child to me, and I was about to lose that child. In having it, I was able to communicate in a way that gave added meaning to my life. It allowed me to know and understand more of what I am really about. I felt as if a part of me was going to be taken away. Helen's plan was to return it to an Aboriginal council, but that did not make me feel any better.

My eyes may close, but I never lose consciousness when I channel. I operate in a different state, aware of here and there at the same time. When I hold the Alcheringa stone, it is very easy for me to get into that state. I will miss it, for I love it dearly. It is my link to the energy of the world of light. I know now that everything is energy. Nothing is really solid.

Gerry had just returned from America, and he and Margaret came to see me. Margaret wanted to ask Alcheringa a question. The sadness that permeated my mood was obvious when they arrived. Gerry suggested that we go out into the sun and walk into the bush for the reading.

I brought out the Alcheringa stone to take with us, told Gerry about the call from Helen Boyd, and said that I would soon deliver the stone back to her at Byron Bay, near Mount Warning.

They both looked at each other, and then at me with eyes that were warm with compassion, yet strangely curious. To my surprise, Gerry took the stone into his hands and carried it as we left the house.

We travelled through the bush for some minutes without talking. I guess I was not in a conversational mood that day. I felt lost and sad.

Gerry finally spoke, "You walk along in the bush with two Koori, and yet you know so little about us."

My heart sank even further, "Yes, that's true."

Gerry stopped and held out the stone to me, "You know more about this stone than you do about us, and now even this is leaving you."

I nodded and lowered my head. I wanted to weep, my eyes ached for the tears to come, but they would not. Why couldn't I cry?

Margaret took my hand and led me to a small clearing. Gerry placed the stone on the ground and we sat around it.

Gerry leaned close to me and almost whispered, "Let me tell you a little about the Koori, so you will know something of us. It will help you to understand our people.

"Long ago, in the timeless time we call the Dreaming, great spirits roamed the Earth, taking the shape of giant animals. Wollumbin, our Creator, the mother/father God, the being who made us, made the mountains, the valleys, the seas, the plains, the rivers and billabongs, the bush land and the red gum forests. He made the clouds, the sky, and the animals too. From the mountains to the sea, the creeks, streams, and rivers were alive with fish, turtles, and wading birds. The land was lush and green with sub-tropical rain forests where medicines grew abundantly in rich fertile soil. In the rain forests, there were majestic eucalyptus gums, Bunya-Bunya pines, and cedars. The Great Spirit Wollumbin made all these things, and then He made his spirit children, our ancestors. He told them to look after and care for the land as they would look after and care for themselves.

"By and by, the spirit children gave birth to many, and different tribes grew up. We had our arguments, like they do in any family, but the thing that all the tribes had in common, the thing that united us all, was the land and our promise to look after it. In return, Wollumbin gave us our totems and beliefs.

"Wollumbin taught us about the animals, about their drinking habits, the ones we could eat and the ones we could not. Wollumbin taught us how to find water in the dry season, and if the water was brackish how to purify it. He also provided us with lots of bush tucker as well. There were Bogong moths, honey ants, kangaroos and wallabies, witchetty grubs and cobra. We had ducks and water hens, fish and turtle, seeds to make damper and lots of different fruits, vegetables, and roots. We had medicines too, and if we weren't sure which one to use, we would just ask Wollumbin.

"Ours was a planned society of hunters and food gatherers who lived in harmony. When we travelled, there was always a good reason for the move. Sometimes we went on walkabout because we had to be at a certain place for a particular ceremony, or to meet up with another tribe, or take our young men through the trials of manhood. We travelled along the Dreaming tracks, following the path shown to us by Wollumbin. We would find our way by telling the stories of the Dreaming. Each mountain and valley, hilltop and plain, was related to something that happened in the Dreaming. If a mountain were in the shape of a dog's hind leg, we'd tell the story of how the dog lost its leg and the path it was travelling before it had the accident. By telling these stories we'd be able to find our way throughout our country.

"In some tribes the Dreaming stories, family histories, and tribal boundaries are engraved on large rocks, or on special stones, or painted on our bodies during ceremony, or on the walls of caves at special places. Some do the same thing in sand or on tree bark. Those of us from eastern Australia, the **Bundjalung** and others, put all of that on our possum-skin cloaks. If we had trouble with another tribe about the law or kinship business, we would just take off our cloaks and spread them on the ground to sort out our problems. Just like any sensible people would do.

"Women had their own ceremonies. There were special places along the Dreaming path where only women were allowed to go, and these sites were just as sacred as the men's. The young girls were taken to the women's site to be taught by the older women all about 'Women's business.' This included their roles as women in the tribe, their responsibilities to their family, their promised husbands, and their roles as mothers. They were shown and taught sacred women's dance and songs. The girls were taught to look after their health, especially during pregnancy, and shown the proper diet for a pregnant woman. They were taught how to space the birth of their babies, so that when the tribe went on walkabout the children would be strong enough to survive the trek.

"The girls were shown how to gather and prepare fruit and vegetables, and special plants used for making medicines and poisons. The poisons were always used in the proper way. They would collect the bark of a certain tree and beat it on rocks by the bank of a creek or billabong, and then cast the pulp into the water. Pretty soon, the fish would float to the surface and we'd collect them. The poison only stunned the fish, never killing anything in the water. There were certain fruit that were poisonous, and the girls were shown how to prepare them so they were safe to eat.

"They were taught about sewing too. When the hunting parties brought their kills back to camp, they would strip off the skin from the kangaroo tails and remove the tendons. We used the tendons as thread for sewing things like possum-skin cloaks. For needles, we used the bone of the kangaroo, which we filed down until it was just the shape we wanted. The thread we used for sewing was also used for making fishing lines and other things as well.

"Our *Gurrahjis* or *Wijans* (shamans) sang the whales into their breeding grounds. They trained the dolphins to round up fish for inter-tribal ceremonies.

"Wollumbin, the Great Spirit, taught us these lessons and many others. We united together as one people, and have lived in harmony with the land since the time Wollumbin made us.

"We know that the time of changes is coming. Margaret wishes to speak with Alcheringa."

Margaret watched me intently as I closed my eyes and called his name, feeling his presence as he entered me and began to speak.

"I am here my dear and I am very pleased that you have called upon me. I have come today with the energy of the Aboriginal Australian spirit, although this place has not always been known as Australia. The people that have been looking after the energy on this land have been here for hundreds of thousands of years. There is much that even they do not know at this moment. We have been giving information to those who work with us, and they are beginning to understand more about their race, their beginnings, and their place of belonging. Is there a question?"

Margaret spoke up, "Can you tell us about the Earth changes that are coming?"

"There has been much talk about Earth changes, and indeed the more of those that are aware, the more can assist for this transition to take place. The purpose is for humans on this Earth to absorb a new energy from the universal source, this is the nature of the transition. Those giving this assistance will make a 'smoother ride,' if I can put it that way.

"The indigenous races from many of the countries that exist on this Earth work with the energy to assist the transition, and you can draw from their knowledge to assist also. You all have the energy of the indigenous races within you. With some, it is a little farther back than others.

"There will be earthquakes and other uprisings in nature. There have already been many and there will be more. Most people will be protected. You should take notice of this fact. This is because those who are in areas that experience change will have moved to another place. I am not suggesting everybody should get up and move, but rather follow his or her inner-guidance. It is important that fear not be experienced, because this puts negative energy into the transition and will not assist at all."

I pushed through Alcheringa's presence to speak, "But if I feel strongly about remaining where I am, what should I do if I hear of possible changes coming to that same area?"

"This confirms what has been said to you my dear. Do as Egarina told you, do not rush out because you hear of other things. Stay where you feel right within your heart. Those that are encouraged to stay at certain points are performing an act that is like holding a rod of light. This actually assists the transition to take place without too much trauma. If there is a contraction in some part of the Earth, this will assist the flow more easily. If there are blockages, these can be released just the same as they are in a human body. This is work that many with the knowledge and knowingness can do to assist mother Earth.

"It is important that the human does not interfere with the body of mother Earth. For, if interfered with, it can cause blockages that will not allow the breathing of energy to come and go with the freedom that it should. I would encourage you not to worry too much about the outcome, you are all here with a knowingness that you are in service, and you are workers that have offered themselves."

Margaret nodded her head in complete understanding as Alcheringa continued.

"I have also committed myself to work and assist with the transition of mother Earth, and the transition of all the indigenous races. If you can spare time to think of this and assist me in my work, I would be greatly appreciative. All you have to do is to send your prayers towards Uluru, and the energy will be gratefully received with love and compassion.

"I thank you my friends, I thank you, and I leave."

"Alcheringa wait," I yelled, "I want to ask you about the stone. I need to know what to do when I give it back." But he was gone.

Margaret moved close and looked into my eyes, staring at me for what seemed like an eternity. She picked up a small stick, then smoothed the soil in front of her with her other hand.

Using the stick, she drew a picture of Uluru with just a small portion showing above the surface.

"Listen closely to what I tell you," she said as she drew a picture of a serpent. "The first born of **Baiame** is the rainbow serpent, which runs under Uluru. The bulk of Uluru is under the ground. From that first birth came many.

"Baiame spells the word God, no more, no less. Baiame reached in himself and took of himself. He breathed love across the land to allow us to be raised from the mother Earth. Baiame gave us the breath of life, and the mother gave the physical and nurtured it. After Baiame created the Earth and the people, he went back to the rivers of the Dreaming.

"Baiame had eight sisters who cared for his temple at the base of Uluru, or *Ayer's Rock*, as the white man knows it. The sisters dedicated their lives to look after his temple. The entrance was through a cave, which is now called the Seven Sister's Cave, still at the base of Uluru, yet above the ground. Within a vortex in the temple, there were two crystal stones that allowed Baiame to move freely from the rivers of the Dreaming to the earthly physical side.

"Now the sun thought himself a clever lad, and was very envious of Baiame. He felt that if Baiame wasn't around, he could rule the world, everyone would have to bow down to him, because he was a magic lad too. So, he thought of a way to stop Baiame from coming to the physical. He would go to the temple, take and destroy the crystal stones, and kill the eight sisters who looked after them. This would prevent Baiame from ever coming back. He thought there was only one entrance to the temple, and the sisters would be unable to escape.

"One day he came through the cave down to the temple below to take the crystal stones and kill the eight sisters. They were blinded by his fire as he began to kill them one by one.

"What he didn't realise was that there was another exit that only the sisters knew about. While seven of the sisters died one by one, the eighth sister grabbed the crystal stones and ran towards the second exit. In her flight, she dropped one of the crystal stones, out of which Baiame arrived to drive the sun away. The eighth sister ran until she sank to the ground saying, 'Baiame I cannot go on any longer' and there she fell.

"Baiame encased her in a crystal like stone under the mountain of crystal which is Wollumbin, or Mount Warning as the white people call it.

"The eighth white sister still holds the crystal stone, and sleeps with it until it is time for her to return and release universal knowledge of humankind. When this happens, the crystal stone will be broken and a new age will begin. When that time comes, the mountain will part, for Wollumbin is a dormant volcano. This is a place of great power to receive spiritual strength and courage from."

Margaret pulled at my hand, "When you travel to Byron Bay, you should make a pilgrimage to Wollumbin at sunrise. If it is foggy when the sun comes up, it will create a rainbow serpent of colour around you. This will be a sign, meaning you have a role to play to reach humanity."

As she spoke, I could see the scene clearly. Wollumbin is the first place the sun hits in Australia every morning. I nodded, yet did not understand the meaning of what she told me. Three days later, I travelled to give the stone back to Helen Boyd.

Looking across the caldera to sacred Wollumbin (Mt Warning)

Wollumbin sparkled with angelic rainbow colours that spread towards the Lighthouse at Byron Bay, where the little ceremony was to take place. The act of handing the stone back was on Mothers Day, a symbol of birth. I was dressed in white.

I arrived early, just to spend time with the stone I guess. Looking across the bay at Wollumbin, Margaret's words echoed in my ears, and I felt as if I were on that mountain in spirit. I thought about all that had taken place since the Alcheringa stone had come into my keeping. There had been a purpose. But I also knew that I was no longer a part of its journey, it was time to give it back. I was aware the event was very special, and that somehow the handing over of the stone was more than just what was happening on the day. Something had been set in motion a long time before.

Standing by the lighthouse, I watched Helen's face as she arrived. She seemed quite fragile and ill. Her doctors had given her only a short time to live and she seemed to know that it was running out quickly. She had always known the Alcheringa stone belonged to the Aboriginal people, and was determined it would be taken back to its rightful place. Helen suggested I sit with the stone before giving it to her, to see if it had a message for me.

On the other side of the lighthouse there was a little park, right next to a cliff over looking the water. I sat on a bench by the edge, placed the stone on my lap, and looked out at Wollumbin in the distance.

My heart was pounding wildly, all I could think about was losing my link with the other side. Well, get it over with.

"Alcheringa?"

"I am very pleased to be here my child, thank you for inviting me."

"Ah, I'm about to give the stone back to Helen. It won't be around for me to handle anymore. How will I be able to contact you? What will I do?"

Alcheringa chuckled, "Did you have the stone with you the first time you went to Kariong?"

Everything stopped, the birds, the sound of the surf, my heart, everything. I thought back to that day. No, I did not have the stone with me. My heart began to beat again and I smiled, "Gee, I guess I didn't."

"My child, you already have the information within you. You are like this rock, this moulded piece of clay that has been infiltrated with information. You too will be able to release that information. It will still be able to come through you as it has always done.

"Everything is energy my child. The energy of this stone carries ancient memories. This stone returned to you from long ago, and you recognised it. The stone helped you to realise your past, and that you could work with us, which you have done most willingly. Now it moves on to its keepers, the Aboriginal people, carrying more than the old memories. It returns carrying the love and compassion that came through you and all that sat with it. The energy of your memories and those of the others is imbued into the stone once again, refreshed and bringing new hope to bond the races of the world together. You no longer need the stone, send it on its way."

The smile on my face disappeared, "Alcheringa, I have started writing a new book and, well to be honest, I am feeling a little frustrated because I would like to do more writing, or receive information, or something. I feel like I am not going to be able to go ahead like I was before. Will you help me, will you advise me?"

"Of course I will assist you, I have all along. Can you accept this my child?"

"Yes, thank you very much. Is there anything else I should know about this book, perhaps something that should be a little clearer?"

"No."

"Is there anything you want to convey to me?"

"There is really nothing to convey my child, it's just that I like to speak through you. Remember that I am practicing every time I speak through you. Do not fret, do not worry, I will assist you. All you need to do is call on me and I will come."

"Thank you Alcheringa."

"Goodbye my child."

He was gone. I stood up and walked back to the lighthouse where Helen waited. Even after the assurance I had just received from Alcheringa, I must confess that I still felt very nervous and a bit sad.

I told Helen I loved the stone, and that I would always feel a part of it. I asked her, when she finally met up with the stone keeper, to give him a green crysophase (var. *Chrysoprase*) stone that I had brought, and tell him that it was from a heart that had cared for the stone.

When she reached for the Alcheringa stone, Helen was not coming from a point of calmness. Her demeanour was one of urgency, as if she needed to get the stone back while there was still time. She put her hands out to receive it quickly. I looked at them and they seemed Aboriginal to me. The skin was the same honey-colour as many of the Aborigines. Helen's eyes were brown the colour of Aborigine eyes. They were eyes that have held the memory of their beginnings down through the ages.

As I handed her the stone, the sadness left me. I knew there would never again be a separation. The feeling was one of knowing the stone represented energy in me and others that would work to unite the star people, and all those who have the star people energy within them. This was a part of the message from the stone.

The stone left my hands, and there was a feeling of completion and calmness. At the same time, there was one of beginning. It was done, the Alcheringa stone was on its way.

Helen intended to return the stone to its rightful owners, and so took it to central Australia. She did not want to hand it over to just anyone, she wanted it to be to the right person, yet she did not know who that person was. She was unable to find the stone keeper and returned with the stone still in her possession.

Although Helen was determined to make the journey back to central Australia and try again, she never made it. The matter was taken out of her hands when her friends, believing she was sick because of the stone, took it to the Aboriginal land council and handed it over. A few days later, Helen died. The land council people, themselves nervous of the stone, quickly wrapped it up, and mailed it to another land council in Alice Springs. They knew it would find its way back to its rightful place.

The book tour finished, I flew to Lord Howe Island, six hundred miles off the coast of New South Wales, to join my husband for a short holiday.

The island group is the remnant of a long extinct volcano that juts out of the sea. It is covered in rainforest and filled with plants that are found nowhere else in the world. The place felt ancient to me, the environment suspended in time. It matched my melancholy mood. It was cold, being winter. For the first few nights, I had trouble sleeping, as did John.

Then, for no apparent reason, John became increasingly obsessed with the idea of climbing Mount Gower, the tallest peak on the island. Our hosts at the vacation lodge took one look at us (we are both in our sixties mind you) and suggested that we try a little walk up Mount Lidgbird, the smaller of the two, as a test, perhaps as far as the cave known as the goat house.

Mountain climbing is not something that I am particularly interested in, but for some reason it seemed that it would be an important day, and that an understanding would be given. So, I went along with the idea.

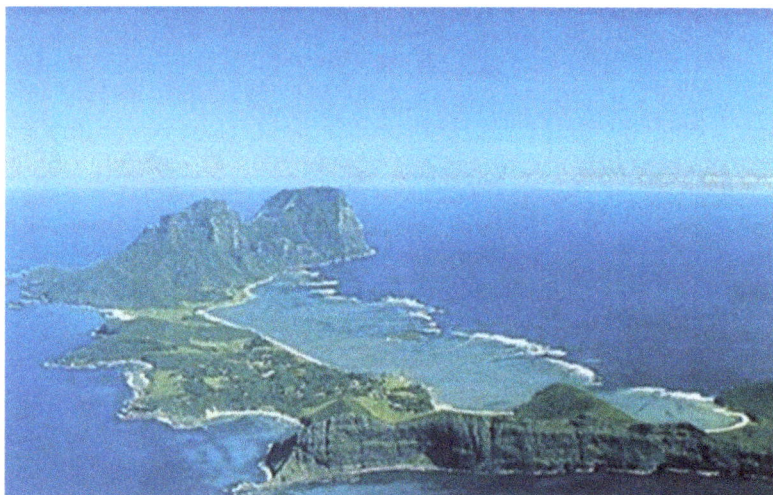

Lord Howe Island - Mt Lidgbird is the nearer of the two tall peaks

The next morning we set off on bicycles to the end of a dirt trail that led to the mountain. From there, we walked through a small rainforest to the foot of Mount Lidgbird. As it turned out, the ascent was not just a walk. It was more like a mountaineering climb.

After what seemed like hours, we finally cleared the tree line to see a beautiful view of one side of the island. Just ahead of us loomed a sheer cliff face. There were rings of iron embedded into the rock with ropes strung between them above a narrow ledge. John encouraged me to move ahead. I felt myself shaking, not with fear, but with the sheer exertion of it all. Well okay, there was some fear.

We climbed along the cliff on the narrow ledge, holding onto the ropes. I felt disoriented and slightly dizzy. Eventually I just had to give it away, so I stopped where I was and asked John do the last part without me. As he moved around the edge of the precipice, I turned and sat on the narrow ledge with my back to it. I grabbed onto some little tufts of grass and held on for dear life.

As I sat on the tiny ledge, I could feel the ancient energy of the place envelope me. It was if I were in a time capsule, as if the energy was from long ago.

I became aware that my soul, or spirit, had not been in this body from its physical birth. It was quite a strange feeling. There had been a near death experience, and two souls had agreed to an exchange.

I was being allowed to take over this body for a reason. It was as if I was a 'walk in' who had come into the physical to do a special task.

The sense of it was more of a knowing rather than something concrete or logical. I remembered finding it difficult coming into this body, it was hard to deal with the energy of it.

I could not quite 'earth' myself. It seemed that there was a reason or a purpose for this, but I could not quite remember.

An eagle soared into view, and then seemed to hover out in front of me in the updraft. It called to me with its raucous voice.

A tremendous feeling of elation came over me and I suddenly felt entirely different. It was like I had been away forever and was coming back with a new energy, an earthing of myself into the physical body. Now it was really I, and not somebody else.

A warm aura settled over me and I felt the presence of Egarina. I called her name. She spoke not through me but in me , "She is not Egarina anymore. Egarina has linked with the Archangels. She is no longer an aspect. This is complicated, but I will try to explain. I cannot come here fully, for I now operate in a different frequency altogether. It's like a cog in a wheel, a place where the third dimension does not fit."

"When did you do this?"

"In your terms, just now, as you earthed into the physical body. Now she is dropping the information down the slippery dip."

"The what?" I could feel her laughing .

"A slippery slide that allows her energy, her messages, to slide into Valerie, and then Valerie repeats the words into the book. Isn't that wonderful?"

"Yeah, I guess so."

"She is able to come through in a very electric way because your energy actually enhances hers, and makes it possible for the aspect that she was then to manifest briefly. This is why, between the two of us, we are able to bring her forth. But that is only the frequency that she was as Egarina. She is not coming from that point anymore. Do you understand?"

"You lost me completely there." Egarina laughed again, and then she sighed.

"There is something I have come to tell you. Almost a million years has passed for the evolution of the little earthling since I first came to this planet. There has been influence down through the ages to help with their evolution.

"When I left my star being body I returned straight away and walked into one of the new creatures. I was able to take on a role as mother and continue to do the work of light and love because the new creatures had been imbued with the crystalline energy.

"I was very much the 'wise-woman' of the tribe. I taught the new ones how to work with the psychic energy that increased knowledge and wisdom, and to use telepathy to communicate.

"The new people did not have the ability to understand technical knowledge. It was easier for them to understand concepts like the lizard people, the snake people, and others that were connected to the reptiles. The furry animals were linked to the race from which they had come. They were all told stories from that point, a little like you would tell stories about animals to children.

"It was from there that the myth of the white sisters was established. This lore was given to the Aboriginal people to help them remember their source. The original story was that the sisters had come from the Pleiades, and when the family of the original ones died, they returned to the Pleiades. They weren't given the full details of the galactic families or races in the earlier days. They were just told that the seven stars represented the Pleiades group.

"The little Aboriginal people could look to the sky, point to the Pleiades system, and see seven stars. They understood the number seven, we taught them this. They even made their own little stories up. They kept the story going amongst their storytellers in various tribes. At times I would manifest to them as a reminder.

"They were also told that one sister from the eighth star would return, the star that was just out of their sight. The idea of the eighth white sister returning was to update their knowledge of understanding, to remind them once again of their beginnings from the Pleiades, and at the same time spread the story and the knowledge of the original mission to Earth. This was promised to happen when the time was right, and that time is now."

"Of course in the bigger plan, the story was to be released not only to the Aboriginal people, but to all those who have their ears open and are ready to hear."

"What about Margaret's Aboriginal story about the eighth white sister being asleep in Wollumbin?" I asked.

"About the time the myth was being told to them, the star people were also teaching the Aboriginal people about the energy of crystals, which they have always used. The crystalline energy protected the star people, and we wanted the Aboriginal people to understand they too were protected by the crystalline energy that was imbued in them. They didn't have the technology or the knowledge as a scientist to understand the structure of crystalline energy, and so we included crystals in the myth and connected to it that way.

"Wollumbin was an active volcano. The people came to know and understand crystals existed on Wollumbin, and that crystals came from the inside of the Earth. It was easy for them to understand other crystals would still be under the great mountain, and so it was told to them the sister lay asleep inside a crystal under the mountain. It was just a way of helping them to understand she was with them, and that she would come forth when the time was right to help them to understand their beginnings.

"The Aboriginal people were very good at holding the original story, but sometimes they got a bit carried away and embellished it. They expanded the story to some degree, which is why there are a number of them that differ. But the common line of all of them is that a sister from the eighth star will come back when time is right to release knowledge. The Aborigine are aware, and they wait."

"How will this knowledge be known?" I asked.

"It is to be through your book my dear one, for I am the eighth white sister. My message is one of hope, one of love and compassion for one another in all races. The people of the world will soon join together, knowing that they are all the same. There will no longer be a reason for them to fight amongst themselves, and there will be peace. My message is of the love from the Source that imbues all.

"The future walks by itself separately, yet beside you. The future can be many different things depending on which track one walks. The future is how you think and feel, and how you imbue the love into yourselves and each other. If all walk with love and compassion for their brothers and sisters, no matter what the colour of their skin, they will create a race of harmony and goodwill.

"Everyone will choose the path on which they walk. They will make the decision individually. There will be those who walk one track and those who walk another. The individual will only walk a track that suits their frequency. At all times the choice is theirs. With the knowledge of the eighth white sister returning, they will hopefully give serious thought to the direction their steps will take, and on what track they will choose."

"But how does one know that they are on the right track?" I asked.

Egarina laughed, "There is no such thing as the right track, it is one's choice about what one feels happy about. We hope our story will help people to make the choice, and realise and gain inner-strength. It is up to them.

"There are many ways to find the god-consciousness within. Your book is not designed for that. The eighth white sister returns to bring knowledge of the existence of many galactic races that are connected to the Source, and to bring knowledge to the races that have been victims, who do not know and understand the Source. Egarina challenges each of them to find the God consciousness within.

"The Golden Age is coming, a rising of frequency amongst all the beings upon this Earth. It is the same for the mother when she is about to produce a child. This is what is happening to mother Earth, her frequency is being raised, she is about to give birth to new children with a raised consciousness.

"Write these words into your book for all to see who will see. It is their decision to accept or not accept. That is the freedom granted by the Creator. I love you my child."

The eagle tilted its wings on the wind and soared away. I stood and felt the wind gusting around my body. I wanted to fly. Below me, the view of the island seemed brighter, the colours more intense. The sound of the wind and the smell of the Earth seemed fresh and new, as if I were experiencing them fully for the first time. I raised my arms to the sky and gave thanks for being alive in the Garden of Eden.

Tears began to flow from my eyes.

John returned around the edge of the precipice looking as if he had just conquered the mountain, "That was fantastic Val, you don't know what you missed up there."

I moved into his arms and sobbed like a child. My tears were the tears of blissful joy.

CHAPTER 11

Valerie, Gerry and Karen
Return to Kariong

shook her head, "The memories have all faded away. I'm left with just the emotions I felt that day and all the other days I remembered the past of the star people. No matter how hard I try to remember, the only thing that comes in are the feelings."

We sat in my study as I sorted through the mound of transcriptions I had typed from all the people who had come to tell their story. My feeling was one of elation. The experience at Lord Howe Island now gave me constant reassurance life was wonderful to behold, every moment was a treasure unto itself, and that I still had a big job to do.

I looked over at Karen, "You still remember giving birth in that rock cradle at Kariong don't you?"

"No, I have the feeling of it, but all the visual memory has gone. I don't know why either. I've tried and tried to see it. The only thing that came to me is something I remembered from many years ago in this life."

"What was that?"

"I was having tea at someone's house, and then I was introduced to a man, Peter I think his name was. As I stood to meet him, the room spun like a wheel from outside to inside. There was a ringing in my ears, like a bell or an urgent buzzing. The feeling stayed with me for several hours.

"When I got home, I was still dizzy and sat down. Then I saw myself in what seemed to be way back in time, because something pointed, or rounded, appeared to be on the back of my head. I thought, oh yeah one of those pointed Elizabethan hats. I was much thinner and wore a flowing dress. I seemed to be on a battlefield, and I had someone lying on my lap. I was distraught about it and thought this must be a brother, or a son, or a husband that's been wounded in this battlefield, and I have rushed out to do something. There was an overwhelming feeling of devastation as I looked down at the thick black hair on his head.

"I am trying to work out what the year was. What was this battle? I saw the number nine, with a smaller zero behind that, and an even smaller zero behind that, then what seemed like other numbers that disappeared into mist or cloud. I looked at the mist and thought 'that must be cannon fire smoke' and wondered whether there were two zeros, or three zeros. Maybe there were more.

"The dream kept reappearing over the years. Sometimes I would remember the afternoon it first happened, and think that I was going back to do all this stuff again. I never figured it out."

I smiled at her, "You still remember Karen, the visual images may be more abstract now, but you remember. Perhaps the feelings and emotions are the most important part. Those reside in the heart."

Someone began beating a drum. I stood, and through the window saw Gerry beating a drum with feathers on it.

Karen stood, "What's happening?"

I opened the window and waved at Gerry.

Gerry walked up to the window, saw Karen, and smiled at her. Then he turned to me with big brown eyes that were friendly and familiar, "I had a dream that we all returned to Kariong."

It took a few seconds for me to react. Most of the time I just flow with events as they happen, not really trying to analyse them. Gerry was waiting.

"Uh," I stuttered, "let me get some things together."

Fifteen minutes later we sped along the highway towards Sydney and Kariong beyond. I was driving. Karen leaned forward to Gerry who sat beside me with the drum.

"Where did you get that?" she asked.

"The Cherokee tribe gave it to me when I was in America," Gerry replied, turning to Karen. He looked at her for a moment, "It's been two years gone now Karen, what have you learned?"

Karen laughed nervously, "I forgot everything. It's all gone."

"She remembers the feelings," I noted.

Gerry turned to me, "That and the Earth are the most important part." He looked back to Karen, "Why did you forget everything?"

I could see Karen's face in the rear view mirror. She looked troubled.

"I don't know," she replied defensively. "What do you remember?"

"Remember what?" Gerry replied, "I've been taught all this stuff since I was a little kid."

"What about that first day at Kariong?"

Gerry smiled, "I remember you and the ship, dying in the sea. There are other little pieces of things from before that. There was an academy where I wore a blue uniform. I wasn't taught any of that, it's what I remember. It's easy for me, I am Koori."

Karen waved her arm, "Well I'm not."

Gerry turned to me, "Has Karen forgotten about having that hairy kid?"

"Aw, Gerry," I pleaded. Karen burst into tears. I looked for a place to stop.

Ahead was a pullover with some nice trees. We stopped and I got out, opened Karen's door, and walked her sobbing towards a little rest area near the trees. Gerry followed.

I looked at Gerry and sighed, then took Karen's hand. "It's okay Karen, you don't remember, so there's no reason to cry."

Karen pointed at Gerry between sobs, "I remember it now, he reminded me." Gerry winked at Karen. "It's better that you do."

Karen sat on a log bench and sniffled. Gerry took my hand, "Let's give her a moment to get back on line."

We moved away and sat on another log bench. "Let's try you now, just relax," said Gerry. "Two years Val, what's been learned?"

The faces of the people who had come into my life to tell their part in this story flashed fresh and clear in my mind. The one who first helped to set the wheels in motion sat next to me looking into my eyes again with that incredible warmth. How wonderful I felt at that moment.

We were all back again with hope and love in our hearts. It was as if we had never parted. A message of love united us again.

Tears flowed from my eyes. I've changed so much in two years; tears come easy to me now "I don't know where to start." I said.

"Start at the beginning," Gerry answered.

"Well, I don't really know what the whole situation is. There is a part I understand. Angels have the power of creation in them. With permission from the Creator, it is they who create physical beings. They all have their own regions to play in. Certain angels turned away from the Creator. This happened billions of years ago, it was almost an accident. These angels created physical beings that were without love, calling them the Draco. The Draco in turn created the reptilians."

Gerry nodded, "The Koori know them as the lizard and snake people."

"You do?"

"Yeah."

"Oh," I continued, "The Draco don't have the light of love and compassion in them because the angels that created them lost it; it was no longer theirs to give."

Gerry nodded again, "The Dreamtime tracks tell us that the lizard and the snake people did not love the earth. Long ago, they came and made war here. These creatures could shift their shape. They took many people from our tribes. We have a teaching to stay close to the elders, to keep the people together for protection from them."

"Well yes," I replied, "that's because the food of the Draco is the consciousness of living creatures. At first, simple life forms were consumed by the Draco to survive. Then they began to consume civilisations of the star worlds."

"Do you mean that the Draco ate our people?" asked Gerry.

"Not the body, just the consciousness within the body", I replied. "I mean, the body died anyway, it's just how the Draco lived."

Karen walked over, "Are these Draco things still around here?"

"No, not exactly." I replied, noting her instant recovery.

"So what happened?" asked Karen.

"The beings of the star worlds were intelligent loving creatures, but they were forced to fight for their survival. Endless wars raged throughout the galaxy. The star worlds tried everything to solve the Draco problem. One was the creation of the planet Earth.

"The plan was to seed the Earth with beings that were born of love and compassion. They would multiply and serve as hosts for the Draco and their creations, as well as a lot of others. Now those without love could experience recurring lives in physical bodies that had love and compassion built into them. This has allowed them to evolve over the last nine hundred thousand years.

"The star people came here and succeeded in making us, the perfect vehicle. All the hate, violence, and madness in humankind allow the vehicle to learn sorrow, compassion, humility, and finally love. The process is a cleansing. That's why our history is the way it is.

"Humans now numbers in the billions. Since our inception, we have numbered in the trillions, giving countless opportunities for incarnation by beings from all over the universe."

"Where do you think this is all going?" asked Gerry.

I took the moment, "Where do you think this is all going?"

Gerry threw his head back and laughed. When he stopped, he viewed me calmly and said, "Well, my people are leaving pretty soon, the cycle is almost complete, although the Aboriginal spirit of the land will always be present."

"What is happening?" asked Karen. Gerry pointed at me for the answer.

"There is a quickening," I replied, "part of it affecting time. Then there is the awakening of love, and those who follow it will enter into an age of peace and harmony."

Gerry raised his hand, "And those who don't?"

I stood. "They won't be able to survive the higher vibration, the speeding up part. It's okay, they'll just incarnate on some other earth-like planet with a lower vibration and continue the journey. Everybody succeeds eventually, the power of love conquers everything in its path."

CHAPTER 12

Alcheringa's Message

We sat next to the Grandmother tree, a huge red gum tree that stood near the entrance to the hieroglyphs. Gerry struck his Cherokee drum and sang to welcome in the presence of Alcheringa. The sound of the drum thundered in my ears.

My body jerked back as Alcheringa came surging in. His presence was much more intense than it had ever been. The voice was loud and my arms waved about.

"I am here, and it gives me great pleasure to welcome all of you at this ancient place. I have been waiting a long time for this day.

"Today the task comes to an end at this site. More will follow, but the work is almost finished in this releasing of the records. So, I thank you sincerely for allowing this to take place. Now many will come to know, for you have done well. There is one last message that will close this chapter.

"There is a new energy coming upon the Earth from the centre of the galaxy that will influence the Earth and all upon it. This is part of the natural cycle that takes place within the universe. There is a lifting of energy, a speeding up in the movement of molecules, atoms, and cells. It is also lifting the consciousness of the people who live on Earth.

"Thus, it is no coincidence that more and more people are starting to think about other aspects of themselves than those that exist in the material world. The energy that is coming is destroying all that is holding people back from knowing that they are of God.

"The separation that is taking place is a division between the shadow and the divine light. People are being lifted into a higher consciousness, and their bodies are slowly being changed. They are beginning to change their diet, their drinking habits, and the way in which they live. They seek fresher air and water. This is all part of growing towards the divine light, the divine energy that is the true part of God.

"As time goes on, people will be making a choice as to whether they wish to go with the God energy, or go in a different direction. If they move with the will of God, the changes that take place will occur easily and they will move into a higher dimension and link with their angelic selves.

"This is freedom, a breaking away from the karmic wheel. Here they can be free of the continual coming back and forth, free of disease, disharmony, and anything that goes against divine light.

"With the lifting that is taking place, the cells will be operating from a frequency that is higher. Already the brain and the physical body are starting to be restructured. It is like a rhythm of musical notes that go back and forth in melody and harmony. Think of it as instruments that harmonise, as musical notes and vibrations that bring sounds of harmony around the Earth. Know that this happens in many places within the universe, and the God in between that links all the notes.

"Many will begin to remember that they are truly light beings, and more than what they appear to be in the physical. Those who choose to remember will go back to the unlimited space of a being of light, a God being.

"All the knowledge and understanding is within everyone, it is just a matter of unlocking the doors to allow those memories to come forth.

"The first and most important thing is to have a desire to want to link with the God energy. From there, all else follows. Some would call this intuition. If you follow this, you will make life easier for yourself. Just focus on that point, do not be afraid, for we come with love in our hearts and wish only to assist.

"Pray within for peace and give thanks to God for helping to bring peace upon this Earth. Feel the words within your heart, and let the words send out their energy. Hold that energy within you at all times.

"If you think and act with love, the karmic action of return feeds it back to you. Put love into every action, it's really very simple. If everybody on the Earth is thinking and acting with love, it will return to them with the power of the God source, and there will be peace throughout the universe.

"That is why all these beings are in the little earthling body, to put the action of love into this realm and share it. Does that make some sense?"

Karen spoke up, "Yes, but why have we done this?"

"Because you committed to do it a long time ago. Each of you has done this. Now Pandora's Box will open up, and its contents will flow out to give an understanding. It will touch many and change their lives, for they will have caught a glimpse of the light.

"That is what this is all about, the conquest of darkness by the light of love."

POSTSCRIPT

The information in this book is presented to you without any claims whatsoever. It is up to you to decide if there is meaning within, and if its message applies to you. If it does, then the book has done its job.

The time and effort of many people provided material for this book. Most of it is not included, as it would result in a very large book. Much of the material channelled from Alcheringa and Egarina is not included for the same reason.

Without the people and the channel, there would be no book. I have changed most of the names to protect their identities. These people provided remarkable clues to events of long ago. Most of them underwent strong emotional reactions when recalling their memories, myself included.

Author's Note: This story was first published in 2002. Alcheringa's last message in this book, while sitting under the Grandmother Tree is beginning to happen now in the year 2020, as he prophesied.

Many had serious doubts about what they were recalling. I had my own in the beginning. The light being Alcheringa, and the marvellous continuity of the readings convinced me otherwise.

Out of all this information has come an understanding of what took place long ago. This is summarised, in part, as

Mothership Reunion at the Alcheringa Property

follows: There were angels who turned away from the light of the Creator. This was almost an accident. It happened billions of years ago.

The fallen angels, like other angels who were steadfast in the light, had the power of creation in them, and they created physical beings. Among these was the Draco.

While the Draco had the light of the Creator within them, they did not have the light of love and compassion. They too multiplied and spread to star worlds around the galaxy.

The food of the Draco was the consciousness of living creatures. At first, small life forms were consumed by the Draco to survive. Then they began to consume beings that were of the star worlds. The star beings fought back for their survival. Endless wars raged throughout the galaxy.

The Draco themselves began to create through what we know as genetic engineering. They created the Reptoid, Dinoid, and other races before that. These beings were enslaved and served as a food source for the Draco. They too multiplied and spread to fill many places throughout the galaxy.

Those of the star worlds sought to solve the problem of the Draco, and the situation of the unfortunate beings the Draco had created. Many efforts were made. Among them was the creation of the planet Earth. This was planned to be a Garden of Eden in a very dark corner of the galaxy. It would be a beacon of shining light. The greater plan was to seed the Earth with physical beings born of love and compassion. These beings would multiply and serve as hosts for those who had never experienced the light. Now these unfortunate beings could come and experience recurring lives in physical bodies that had the light of love and compassion inbuilt. This would allow them to evolve.

During the early development of the Earth, long before being seeded with physical beings of light and love, it was taken over by Reptoid and Dinoid cultures under the guidance of the Draco. For millions of years these races occupied the Earth, and created among them the dinosaurs and other life forms. These creatures were initially used as a food offering to the Draco, to spare the Reptoids themselves from being used as food. Out of this creation came a competition between the Reptoid and Dinoid to see who could create the biggest and most violent reptiles.

The dinosaurs over-ran the Earth, much to the concern of other life forms in the galaxy. Beings from the star worlds came to the Earth to observe, entering the oceans to become whales, and continue their observation.

After protracted negotiations between the Draco, and what had become the galactic council of the star worlds, it was realised that the Draco were not willing to relinquish their control of the planet Earth, or the creatures that lived upon it. The star world race known as the Lion People were sent in to change the environment of the Earth in order to rid the planet of the dinosaurs.

The rock known as 'Uluru' was sent to Earth, by the Lion People, and produced the cataclysmic forces that ended the age of the dinosaur. Uluru, wrapped in ice when it first came, had a second mission – it also brought with it genetic material to allow the evolution of warm-blooded beings with hair.

Millions of years later, the Reptoids, being rather brilliant in genetics, took this material, and the genetic material of the **Ceteans**, and created a warm-blooded mammal with hair, the upstanding ape. The new creature was initially used as a food offering to the Draco, as the Reptoid and Dinoid cultures had lost the dinosaur as an offering. Later, the upstanding ape-like beings were also used to mine gold for the Draco.

The Draco discovered that by ingesting white powder gold they became able to travel inter-dimensionally. Eventually the Draco moved on to another dimension, and at last gave the Reptoids and Dinoids their freedom. The upstanding ape-like creatures were allowed to develop on their own, becoming a brutish weapon-wielding race. The Reptoids still maintained a form of mind control over them, calling them in when needed.

The galactic council finally asserted itself and negotiated the departure of the Reptoids and Dinoids from planet Earth. The Reptoids really had no choice, for the Lion Warriors could quite easily destroy them all. The Dinoids moved on soon afterwards.

The Draco were aware of the plan and thought otherwise. A Draco contingent came to Earth and resumed control through the Reptoid leaders.

A grand mission was mounted in the Pleiades to transport fifty thousand star people in a huge mother ship to the planet Earth. The object was to slowly integrate a pioneer colony onto the planet. The Earth itself was a hostile environment for the star people, so they planned to modify themselves genetically to be able to spread across the planet, providing a new race with love and compassion inbuilt. This race would allow the souls of Draco, Reptoid, and Dinoid cultures to incarnate into them and evolve.

Upon arrival, the mission was destroyed by the Reptoids, under the control of the Draco, leaving only ninety survivors who were cast onto the planet.

The Reptoids were perfectly aware of the consequences of their actions. Some returned to their native star systems. Others remained on the Earth. A few went underground. The Draco moved on to another dimension.

The star people who survived struggled to endure the hostile environment of the Earth. A few Reptoids, who had defected from their society, after realising the cruelty of the attack, assisted them.

Five years later, a mission of Lion Warrior ships came to Earth and destroyed the Reptoid settlements, leaving only those that had gone underground.

The survivors of the mother ship chose to stay on the Earth. There really was no choice, for the Earth had changed them forever. They were eventually successful in creating the beginnings of the human race, a new race of beings with the light of love and compassion inbuilt.

This race now numbers in the billions. Since the dawn of their inception, they have numbered in the trillions, giving countless opportunities for incarnation by beings from all over the universe.

For the next nine hundred thousand years, human beings served as hosts for the souls of Draco, Reptoid, Dinoid, and Star World Cultures.

All the hate, madness, and violence that has come out of humankind since that time has served as a vehicle to learn love, sorrow, compassion, and humility. The process in one of cleansing, and this is the reason why our history is the way it is. Things are now changing in the star worlds.

The cycle has almost completed. The time draws near for an awakening. Soon a new golden age will dawn upon the Earth, and those who choose to follow the light of love will enter an age of peace, harmony, and love.

Those that do not choose to follow the light of love will be unable to survive in the new and higher vibration, and will incarnate in another place, perhaps like the Earth, to continue the upward journey to love. They too will eventually succeed, for the power of love eventually conquers everything in its path.

This book is dedicated to the light being known as *Alcheringa*, and to the ancient Aboriginal Spirit of the Earth.

With endless love and gratitude to my husband John, who is very much a part of this story, to our family for their patience and encouragement, and to the star people incarnate who came forth with memories, and were brave enough to share their experiences.

With endless love and gratitude to friends and light workers Helen Vincent, Gerry Bostock, Pauline Godfrey, Chris Bible, Simon Weir, Maurice Adams, Jon and the two Taras, Fergus Anderson, Tim Budden, John and Rosemary Butterworth, Gillian Young, Helen Smythe, Margaret McCann, Rob, Antoinette, Isabella & Christian Sampson, Hazel Rex, Bob Findlay, Lorna

Cuneo, Susan Malloy, Helen Newnham, Peter Robb, David Austin, Belinda Pate, Bob & Jan Wright, Kelvin & Arlene Perks, Mary Marks-Chapman, Alex Toohey and John Mangion. Thank you for your faith, patience, and contribution.

With endless love and gratitude to Simon Weir and Bob Wright for their art, giving the reader a sense of how people from the stars looked nine hundred thousand years ago.

With endless love to the little stone that has been returned safely to the Elders at Alice Springs.

Holy Spirit wanted me to work with Bill Oliver, who took the time to assist me writing this very complex story. Thank you Bill and a big thank you to Alcheringa from both of us for introducing us to this extraordinary story held within our OVERSOUL

In memory of Helen Boyd 1938 – 1997

In memory of Gerry Bostock 1942 – 2014

About the Author

Valérie is a star lady who was not born into her earth body, first arranged by the Karmic Board from Andromeda Galaxy M31. She has been to Earth many times coming as one of the 144,000 starpeople who are here, in earth bodies, to assist the raised consciousness that leads to the alignment of a core of suns to the Creator Central Sun and Earth's new birth into the Golden Age.

Her Mission is to speak of a Sacred Alcheringa Stone, the seven sisters in the Pleiades, and how Alcheringa, the Light Being Creator Ancestor, speaks through her voice box telling of early evolution of Earth and Creation of the **first Humans**. The Australian Aborigine who carry the original up-grade of our DNA to many changes, thereafter, to the Human that we all are now.

Her husband John, also from the stars, had agreed to come to Earth and share her life to assist her remembering their many lifetimes together here on this planet Earth.

They travelled to many sacred places around the world, unearthing hidden aspects of their story. Such as the Egyptian Pyramids, Magdalene and Jesus, The Cathars at Montsegur, The Knights Templars, Jehanne d' Arc and Mr Charles Dickens, to name just a few.

And the extraordinary story of The Sacred Alcheringa Stone from the stars, and its role in revealing the story of the creation of the FIRST HUMANS, a body of Divine Light overlaying our earth body, with the aid of the star people from the Pleiades. Recorded in her book **STARLADY.**

THIS BOOK *Alcheringa - When the First Ancestors were Created* is a record of thirty-three humans who remember being Starpeople and contributed to telling the story of the first humans. There have been hundreds, maybe thousands, who have since advised they are part of this story. Alcheringa, from the World of Light, is the male part of Valerie's oversoul.

Alcheringa from another world placed this image of himself as the Ancient, Creator Ancestor onto Valerie's computer.

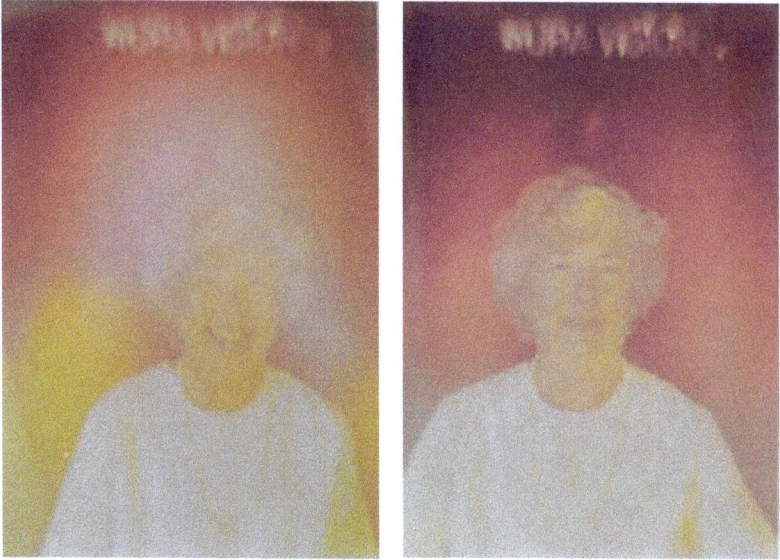

Valerie calling upon Alcheringa in 1994
His wings can be seen in the right-hand image